Budget Saving Meals
COOKBOOK
by Donna M. Paananen

Ideals Publishing Corp.
Milwaukee, Wisconsin

CONTENTS

ISBN 0-89542-620-X

COPYRIGHT © MCMLXXX BY DONNA M. PAANANEN
PUBLISHED BY IDEALS PUBLISHING CORPORATION
MILWAUKEE, WISCONSIN 53226
ALL RIGHTS RESERVED. PRINTED AND BOUND IN U.S.A.
PUBLISHED SIMULTANEOUSLY IN CANADA

Whole Wheat Sesame Seed Bread

Breakfasts and Breads

Cereals and grains are relatively low-cost additions to our diet—especially when they are homemade. Don't underestimate the importance of breads and cereals in your diet; nutritionists remind us to have four servings of these foods daily.

Braided Garlic Bread

      1 cup yogurt (or milk, soured
          with 1 tablespoon vinegar)
      2 tablespoons honey
    ¼ cup water
    ¼ cup vegetable oil
    2½ cups unbleached white flour
      2 packages active dry yeast (5 tablespoons)
      1 teaspoon salt
      3 cloves garlic, minced
    1½ to 2 cups whole wheat flour

Heat first four ingredients in a small pan until very warm (115°). Place white flour, yeast (at room temperature), salt, and garlic into a warmed mixing bowl and pour warm liquid over flour mixture. Blend at low speed with mixer until all ingredients are moistened. Continue to beat at medium speed for 3 minutes. Stir in whole wheat flour with a wooden spoon until soft dough is formed. Turn out onto a well-floured board and knead until smooth (8 to 10 minutes). Place dough in a greased bowl, turn once, and cover. Let dough rise in a warm place for 1 hour or until doubled in bulk. Punch down dough and divide into 3 equal parts. Form each part into long, smooth rolls. Join them securely at the top and braid carefully. Pinch ends together. Place braid on a well-greased baking sheet, cover and let rise in warm place until double, about 30 minutes. Preheat oven to 400° and bake bread for about 25 minutes or until golden. Remove from baking sheet, and, if desired, brush crust with melted butter. Yield: 1 large loaf.

Whole Wheat Sesame Seed Bread

      2 packages active dry yeast
      1 tablespoon honey
      2 cups lukewarm milk
      3 cups whole wheat flour
      1 to 1½ cups unbleached flour
      1 teaspoon salt
    ½ cup wheat germ
    ½ cup sesame seeds
      2 tablespoons vegetable oil

Dissolve yeast and honey in milk. Stir in 2 cups whole wheat flour and beat thoroughly. Stir in 1 cup of unbleached flour vigorously. Add salt, wheat germ, sesame seeds, and vegetable oil. Add the final cup of whole wheat flour and enough unbleached flour to make a workable dough. Turn onto a lightly-floured surface and knead 8 to 10 minutes or until smooth. Place dough in a greased bowl, turn to coat all sides. Cover with a towel. Let rise in a warm place (85°) for approximately 1 hour. Punch down and shape into 2 loaves. Place loaves into greased 8½ x 4½ x 2⅝-inch loaf pans. Cover and let rise in warm place for about 30 minutes or until doubled. Bake at 350° for approximately 35 minutes or until done. Yield: 2 loaves.

Super Zucchini Bread

      3 cups unbleached flour
    1¼ cups raw wheat germ
      1 cup raisins
      1 cup chopped nuts (or less)
      1 tablespoon baking powder
      2 teaspoons cinnamon
      1 teaspoon salt
      2 eggs
    1¼ cup brown sugar, firmly packed
    ⅔ cup vegetable oil
      2 teaspoons vanilla
      3 cups grated zucchini, drained

Preheat oven to 350°. In medium bowl, mix together dry ingredients. In a separate bowl, beat eggs until light colored; beat in sugar until dissolved. Add oil and vanilla. Fold in zucchini. Gradually stir in flour mixture until thoroughly blended. Pour into 2 greased 8½ x 4½ x 2⅝-inch loaf pans. Bake for 1 hour or until done. Cool in pan for 10 minutes before removing to wire racks. Yield: 2 loaves.

Hilda Blackford's Raisin-Nut Bread

    2 cups raisins
    2 teaspoons baking soda
    2 cups boiling water
    1 cup brown sugar, firmly packed
    2 tablespoons butter
    1 teaspoon salt
    3 eggs
    1 teaspoon vanilla
    4 cups unbleached flour
    1 cup chopped nuts
    1 pound fresh cranberries, chopped, optional

Mix raisins, baking soda, boiling water, brown sugar, butter, and salt together and let sit for 2 hours or overnight. Preheat oven to 350°. Add the rest of the ingredients, stirring thoroughly until well-blended. Pour into well-greased loaf pan. Bake for 1 hour or until done. Yield: 1 loaf.

Variation: Replace 2 cups flour with 2 cups rolled oats and add ½ teaspoon baking powder.

Bara Brith (Welsh tea bread)

    2 tablespoons lemon juice
   1½ cups milk
   3½ cups whole wheat flour
    1 teaspoon baking powder
    1 teaspoon baking soda
    ½ teaspoon cinnamon
    ½ teaspoon mace
    ½ teaspoon ground ginger
    ½ teaspoon ground cloves
    1 teaspoon salt
    ½ cup shortening
    ½ cup brown sugar, firmly packed
    ¾ cup currants
    ¾ cup raisins
    1 tablespoon grated lemon rind
    1 tablespoon old-fashioned molasses

Preheat oven to 350°. Stir lemon juice into milk and set aside to clabber. Stir dry ingredients together thoroughly. Cut in shortening with a pastry blender until mixture resembles crumbs. Mix in brown sugar, currants, raisins, and lemon peel thoroughly. Make a well in the center of the flour mixture and pour in the milk and molasses. Mix batter until all ingredients are well moistened and blended. Pour batter into a well-greased 9 x 5 x 3-inch loaf pan. Bake 1 hour or until pick inserted in center comes out clean. Cool in pan on wire rack for 10 minutes; before removing from pan. Serve thinly sliced and buttered. Usually better the second day. Yield: 1 loaf.

Apple Cider Bread

    1 cup apple cider
    2 eggs
    ¼ cup vegetable oil
    1 cup cooked or canned winter squash
       or pumpkin purée
   ⅔ cup brown sugar, firmly packed
    2 tablespoons grated orange rind
   1½ cups unbleached flour
    ½ cup raw wheat germ
    2 teaspoons baking powder
    ¼ teaspoon baking soda
    ½ teaspoon salt
    ¼ teaspoon cinnamon
    ¼ teaspoon nutmeg
    ¼ teaspoon cloves
    ½ cup chopped walnuts

Place apple cider in a stainless steel, glass, or enameled pan over high heat and reduce to ¼ cup. Cool. Preheat oven to 350°. Beat eggs with vegetable oil; stir in purée, sugar, rind, and cider. Mix together all dry ingredients except nuts. Fold the wet ingredients into the dry ingredients carefully until just blended. Stir in the nuts. Pour into a well-greased 8½ x 4½ x 2⅝-inch loaf pan and bake on the middle shelf for 1 hour or until tester inserted in the center comes out clean. Cool completely on a wire rack before removing from pan. Can be frozen. Yield: 1 loaf.

Too many of us continue to underestimate the importance of breakfasts—even when nutritionists stress the fact that it is the most important meal of our day.

With a little planning ahead, breakfast need not consist of expensive cereal from a box or sweet rolls wrapped in plastic. Vary food choices and still get one-third of the total protein for the day by eating a thrifty but nutritious, breakfast.

There are several methods which can be used to help bread dough rise. One method is to place the bowl over the pilot light on a gas stove. Another is to place the bowl near a radiator. Perhaps the best is to place a pan of very hot water on the lower shelf of the oven, then put the dough on the top shelf and close the door. This method promotes a steadily rising dough.

Breakfasts and Breads

Buckwheat Pancakes or Waffles

- 1 cup buckwheat flour
- 1 teaspoon baking powder
- ½ teaspoon salt
- 1 cup milk
- 1 egg, beaten
- 1 tablespoon honey
- 2 tablespoons melted butter or margarine

Mix dry ingredients together thoroughly. Stir in rest of ingredients in order, mixing well after each addition. Pour by ladlefuls onto greased, hot griddle or, following manufacturer's specifications, into waffle iron. Yield: approximately 10 pancakes or 4 waffles.

Note: Extra pancakes or waffles can be frozen until needed. Toast, frozen, in toaster until heated through.

Herbed Bread

- 2 packages active dry yeast
- 2 cups lukewarm water
- 2 tablespoons honey
- 2 teaspoons salt
- 2 tablespoons soft butter or margarine
- 1½ tablespoons crumbled, dry oregano
- 4 to 5 cups whole wheat flour or a combination of unbleached white and whole wheat flour
  Romano or Parmesan cheese

Mix yeast and water together in a large bowl. Stir in honey. Add salt, margarine, and oregano. With an electric beater, beat in 2 cups flour at low speed until thoroughly blended. Add 1 more cup; beat until smooth. With a wooden spoon, gradually beat in rest of flour until a workable dough is formed. Turn out onto a lightly floured board and knead until smooth. Place in a greased bowl; turn to grease all sides. Cover with a towel and let rise in a warm place (85°) for 1 hour or until doubled in bulk. Punch down and shape into a round loaf. Place on a well-greased baking sheet and sprinkle surface with Romano or Parmesan cheese. When nearly doubled in size, bake at 375° for approximately 1 hour or until done. Yield: 1 loaf.

"Staff" as used in "bread is the 'staff' of life" is defined by Webster as "a support." Could you call the bread your family eats the "support" of life? Make certain the bread your family eats can support life by making it of highly nutritious ingredients.

Puffed Pancakes

- 2 cups whole wheat or unbleached flour
- ¼ cup nonfat dry milk powder
- 2 teaspoons baking powder
- 1 teaspoon salt
- 1½ cups milk
- ¼ cup vegetable oil
- 2 egg whites, beaten until stiff

Mix dry ingredients together in a large bowl. Make a well in the center. Pour milk and oil into the well and mix until dry ingredients are just moistened. Gently fold beaten egg whites into the batter. Pour by ¼ cupfuls onto a lightly greased, hot griddle. Bake until bubbles form and begin to break on the surface and sides begin to look done. Turn and brown the other side. Yield: 16 3-inch pancakes.

Granola

- 6 cups rolled oats
- 1 cup whole wheat flour
- 1 cup raw wheat germ
- 1 cup Flaked Coconut (page 60)
- ½ cup sunflower seeds (or more)
- ½ cup soy nuts, peanuts, *or* other inexpensive nuts
- ½ cup vegetable oil
- ½ cup honey
- ⅓ cup water
- ½ teaspoon salt
- 1 teaspoon vanilla
- 1 cup raisins, prunes, dates, currants, or other fruit available

Preheat oven to 350°. In a very large bowl, mix together oats, flour, wheat germ, coconut, seeds, and nuts. In a separate container, mix together the rest of the ingredients except raisins. Pour wet ingredients over dry; mix thoroughly until well blended. Spread mixture onto two well-greased baking sheets. Bake for 30 minutes or until golden, stirring regularly. When thoroughly cool, stir in fruit. Store in an airtight container. Serve with milk, yogurt, fruit, etc., as a breakfast cereal or as an ingredient in cookies, breads, or snack items. Yield: approximately 3 quarts.

Appetizers and Savory Snacks

Packaged snack items often put a huge dent in the family food budget, so why not make your own inexpensive snacks at home and let your family share in the enjoyment. Freshly-popped popcorn, for example, is not only inexpensive, but calorie counters will be happy to know, there are only 200 calories in three cups of plain popcorn! Homemade crackers can be fun to make as well as economical. Roasted pumpkin, squash, and sunflower seeds are always a favorite with children. Take a walk in the woods and bring home nuts to munch on. Cheese makes a nutritious snack, and, bought in bulk, saves you money. Extra cheese can be frozen and used for cooking. And, vegetables from the garden always offer the best budget-saving, nutritious appetizers and snacks.

Sauerkraut Balls

- 2 tablespoons butter or margarine
- 1 small onion
- 1 clove garlic
- ¼ cup cooked ham
- ¼ cup beef stock or bouillon
- 2 tablespoons whole wheat flour
- 1½ cups sauerkraut, well drained
- 1 tablespoon fresh parsley
- 1 egg
- ⅔ cup milk
- ¼ cup non-instant powdered milk
  Extra whole wheat flour
  Raw wheat germ
  Vegetable oil for deep-fat frying

Melt butter in heavy skillet. Grind onion and garlic and cook in butter until onion is transparent. Grind ham and stir into onion mixture. Heat thoroughly, add beef stock and heat again just to boiling. Stir in flour and immediately reduce heat. Stir constantly, adding more flour if necessary, until mixture is very stiff. Grind sauerkraut and parsley, squeezing dry before stirring into ham mixture in skillet. Blend thoroughly. Cover and refrigerate. Beat egg and milks together in a small bowl. When sauerkraut mixture is cold, roll into small balls. Roll in whole wheat flour, then dip in egg-milk mixture. Roll in wheat germ. Dry for 10 minutes then fry in deep fat heated to 350° to 360° until nicely browned. Sauerkraut balls may be frozen. If frozen, bake without thawing on an ungreased baking sheet at 350° until hot. Yield: approximately 2 dozen.

Parslied Liver Paté

- 6 slices bacon
- 1 cup chopped onion
- ½ pound pork sausage
- 1 pound liver, trimmed
- ⅓ cup milk
- 6 fresh sage leaves
  Salt
  Freshly ground black pepper
- ⅔ cup minced parsley

Cook bacon in a large skillet until crisp. Drain on paper toweling. Pour off excess fat. Sauté onion in fat until transparent. Add pork sausage, break into bits, and cook until thoroughly browned. Remove onion and sausage. Pour off excess fat. Wash liver in milk and slice, if necessary, to insure quicker cooking. Sauté liver in the same pan pork sausage was cooked in until done. Place all the above ingredients in a food processor fitted with the steel blade or in a meat grinder. Add sage and grind until fine. Taste and correct seasonings. Form into a ball and sprinkle with parsley. Chill until serving time; serve surrounded by crackers or small rounds of bread. Yield: 1½ pounds.

Fresh Fruit Cup

- 1 cup watermelon balls
- 1 cup canteloupe balls
- 1 cup honeydew melon balls
- 1 cup sliced banana, sprinkled with lemon juice
- 1 cup cubed pineapple
- 1 cup hulled strawberries
- 1 cup fresh peach slices
- 1 cup orange slices
- 1 cup seedless green grapes
- 1 cup blueberries
- 1 cup bing cherries
  Sugar, optional
- ⅓ cup rum, Cointreau, curacao, sherry, or apple juice
  Mint leaves

Choose from the above fruits, selecting a total of six cups. Mix fruits, sugar lightly, if desired, and chill, covered. Just before serving, pour liqueur or juice over fruit. Serve in frosted glass bowl, scalloped melon shell, or in individual, stemmed sherbet glasses. Garnish with mint leaves. Yield: 6 servings.

Cornish Pasties

3½ cups sifted, unbleached flour
½ cup ground suet
1 teaspoon salt
¾ cup margarine
½ cup cold water

All ingredients must be *cold*. With a pastry blender, blend flour, suet, salt, and margarine together until mixture resembles crumbs. Add water and mix lightly until dough holds together. Knead on a lightly floured board or cloth for a few moments until dough is smooth. Divide into 2 balls and chill until dough is firm (approximately 20 minutes). Roll out 1 ball of dough at a time on a lightly floured board until it is a little thicker than ⅛-inch. Cut with a 2½-inch round cookie cutter. Cover and refrigerate rounds until ready to fill them. Spread a small amount of the filling on half of each round. Fold the other half over and seal edges well. Place fill pasties on an ungreased baking sheet and bake 15 minutes at 375°; lower heat to 350° and bake 30 minutes or until pasties are golden. Yield: approximately 3 dozen.

Filling

1 cup raw potatoes, pared and sliced
½ pound choice stewing beef, cut in small pieces
4 tablespoons chopped onion
2 tablespoons ground suet
½ cup parsley, chopped fine
½ cup diced turnip
½ cup diced carrots
1 teaspoon salt
Freshly ground black pepper

Mix ingredients together lightly,

Sesame Seed Crackers

1 tablespoon lemon juice
½ cup milk
1⅓ cups unbleached flour
¼ cup rolled oats
¼ cup bulgur (cracked wheat)
3 tablespoons sesame seeds
½ teaspoon salt
½ teaspoon baking soda
3 tablespoons margarine, melted

Stir lemon juice into milk and set aside to clabber. Combine dry ingredients in a bowl. Stir in milk and butter. Knead the dough until ingredients are thoroughly mixed. Form into a ball and chill, wrapped, for about an hour. Preheat oven to 350°. Roll out dough about ⅛-inch thick on a well-floured surface with well-floured rolling pin. Cut with a round biscuit or cookie cutter into 2-inch rounds and place on well-greased baking sheets. Prick a pattern on the crackers with a fork and bake for 10 to 12 minutes or until golden and crisp. Cool on a wire rack. Yield: approximately 3 dozen.

Sardine Paste

1 3¾-ounce can sardines in oil, drained, skinned, and boned
1 tablespoon minced onion
2 tablespoons mayonnaise
1 teaspoon lemon juice
1 teaspoon Worcestershire sauce
½ teaspoon chili powder
1 hard-cooked egg, shelled and chopped
Thin slices bread or toast

Mash sardines with a fork. Stir in all ingredients except bread until thoroughly blended. Trim crusts and flatten bread with a rolling pin. Spread with paste. Roll bread slices, fasten with toothpicks, and place on a lightly greased baking pan. Bake in a 400° oven until bread is toasted and appetizer is heated through. Spread may also be served on buttered toast. Yield: ½ cup.

Wheat Germ Sticks

1 teaspoon baking powder
2 tablespoons soy flour
¾ cup raw wheat germ
½ cup whole wheat pastry flour
1 tablespoon minced chives
⅛ teaspoon salt
¼ cup margarine
2 tablespoons milk
1 egg white
¼ cup raw wheat germ

Mix first six ingredients together; cut in margarine until mixture resembles crumbs. Stir in 1 tablespoon milk and egg white lightly but thoroughly with a fork. Shape into a ball. Preheat oven to 400°. Roll out dough on a well-floured board with a well-floured pin to about ⅛-inch thickness. Cut dough into 36 sticks approximately 3½-inches long. Brush sticks with final tablespoon milk and roll in wheat germ. Place on ungreased baking sheets and bake for about 6 minutes or until golden. Yield: 3 dozen.

Raw vegetables in season or out of the garden are a penny-pincher's dream: no energy is needed to cook them; they are highly nutritious yet inexpensive; and they are low in calories.

Hot Cheese Rounds

¾ cup margarine
⅓ cup blue cheese
½ cup shredded sharp Cheddar cheese
    or similar cheese
1 garlic clove, minced
1 teaspoon minced chives
1 teaspoon minced parsley
1 teaspoon baking powder
1 cup whole wheat flour
1 cup unbleached flour

Cream together margarine and cheeses. Add garlic, chives, parsley, and baking powder. Stir thoroughly. Add flour slowly, mixing thoroughly. Shape into 2 rolls, each about 1½ inches in diameter. Chill well. Preheat oven to 375°. Slice rounds ¼-inch thick and place on well-greased baking sheets. Bake 8 to 10 minutes or until golden. Serve hot. Yield: approximately 5 dozen.

Stuffed Cucumber

½ cup cottage cheese
2 tablespoons parsley
1 tablespoon chives
1 clove garlic
½ teaspoon curry powder (or more, to taste)
    Salt
    Freshly ground black pepper
1 long, European cucumber, unpeeled
    Lettuce, parsley, optional

Place cottage cheese, parsley, chives, and garlic in blender; blend until smooth. Season to taste. Slice cucumber lengthwise and scoop out centers slightly. Spoon cottage cheese mixture into centers and chill thoroughly. To serve, slice each cucumber half into eighths or smaller and serve on a plate garnished with lettuce or parsley, if desired. Yield: approximately 16 servings.

Party Puffs

½ cup margarine
1 cup water
1 cup unbleached flour
4 eggs at room temperature

Preheat oven to 400°. Heat water and margarine to a rolling boil in a heavy saucepan. Quickly stir in flour with a wooden spoon. When mixture looks smooth and forms a ball, stir faster until spoon will leave a smooth imprint on the paste. Remove from heat and add eggs, one at a time, stirring vigorously after each addition. When all eggs are added and mixture is smooth but not slippery, drop dough by slightly rounded teaspoonfuls onto an ungreased baking sheet. Bake 25 to 30 minutes or until puffed and golden. Slice puffs and remove any uncooked bits inside, readying the puffs to be filled. Spoon Filling into puffs. If not served immediately after filling, puffs may be reheated in a 350° oven for about 10 minutes or until heated through. Yield: approximately 50.

Variations: Make herbed puffs by adding 1 teaspoonful of dill seeds, garlic salt, poppy seeds, celery seeds or caraway seeds to the water and margarine combination. Or make cheese puffs by adding ¾ cup grated Swiss, sharp Cheddar, or a combination of Swiss and Parmesan cheese to the warm paste before forming into the puffs.

Filling

2 tablespoons margarine or butter
2 tablespoons unbleached flour
1 cup milk
¼ cup minced onion
1 small bay leaf
1 6½-ounce can tuna fish, drained

Melt margarine in a heavy saucepan; stir in flour and blend for about 5 minutes over very low heat. Add milk gradually, stirring to keep smooth. Finally, add onion and bay leaf and simmer, stirring regularly, until thick. Remove bay leaf. Stir in tuna and heat thoroughly.

Taramasalata

1 2-ounce jar red caviar (lumpfish roe)
3 slices dry bread
¼ cup milk
2 tablespoons lemon juice
½ cup vegetable oil
2 tablespoons minced onion
2 cloves garlic, minced

Soak caviar in water for about 5 minutes to remove salt. Drain. Soak bread in milk; squeeze dry. Place caviar, bread, and remaining ingredients in blender and blend until smooth, light and creamy. Spread on buttered bread rounds or toast or use as a dip for celery sticks, cucumber or green pepper slices, etc. Yield: 1¼ cups.

Soups and Stews

Whether it's a frosty soup on a hot summer's day or a steamy stew on a blustery winter evening, good soups soothe the soul when the pocketbook has little in it.

Potato Soup

- 3 cups water
- 4 cups peeled, sliced potatoes
- 3 cups chopped onion
- 2 bay leaves
  Freshly ground black pepper
- 1½ cups milk
- ½ cup nonfat dried milk powder
- 2 tablespoons margarine or butter
  Salt
  Chopped chives

In a large soup kettle, bring water, potatoes, onion, bay leaves, and pepper to boil; reduce heat and simmer, covered, for about 20 minutes or until potatoes are tender. Stir in milks and margarine. Taste and correct seasonings. Heat but do not boil. Serve garnished with chopped chives. Yield: 6 to 8 servings.

Bean Soup

- 2 cups (16 ounces) dried navy beans
- 2½ quarts water or vegetable
  cooking liquids or thin broth
- 1 meaty ham bone (approximately 1½ pounds)
- 1 cup chopped onion
- 2 cups chopped carrot
- 2 cloves garlic, minced
- 1 cup chopped celery
- 1 bay leaf
- 2 tablespoons parsley
- ¼ teaspoon ground allspice
- ½ teaspoon freshly ground black pepper
  Salt

Rinse and sort beans. Place in a large soup kettle with water. Bring to boil, reduce heat, and simmer 2 minutes. Remove from heat; let stand, covered, 1 to 2 hours. Add ham bone, vegetables, and seasonings, except salt. Simmer, covered, for 1 hour or until beans are tender. Remove ham bone and slice off meat. Dice meat and add to soup. Reheat until soup is at serving temperature. Taste and correct seasonings before serving. Yield: 8 servings.

Cambrian Stew

- 3 pounds lamb necks or shoulder, cut up (with bones)
- ½ cup whole wheat flour
- ½ teaspoon salt
  Freshly ground black pepper
- 8 to 10 young, small carrots, scrubbed
- 8 to 10 young, small white onions, peeled
- 3 celery stalks, sliced
- 1¼ cups vegetable or other stock
- 1¼ cups beer
- 6 parsley sprigs
- 1 bay leaf
- 1 sprig thyme or ⅛ teaspoon dry
  Parsley

Remove any bone splinters from meat. Mix flour, salt, and pepper in a paper bag. Drop meat pieces in and coat with flour mixture. Place pieces into large saucepan or Dutch oven. Add vegetables, stock, beer, and herbs. Bring mixture to a boil; skim surface and simmer, covered, 1½ to 2 hours or until meat is tender. (If desired, remove bones from the meat and cut meat into bite-size pieces at this point.) Taste and correct seasonings. Serve garnished with chopped parsley. Yield: 6 servings.

Split Pea Soup

- 1 ham hock or meaty ham bone
- 1 pound split peas, rinsed and sorted
- 3 quarts water
- 5 slices lean bacon, chopped
- 1 carrot, chopped
- 1 cup chopped onion
- ¼ cup parsley
- ½ teaspoon thyme
- 2 bay leaves
- ½ cup green part of leeks or green onion
  Salt
  Freshly ground black pepper

Place ham hock, split peas, and water in a large soup kettle and bring to boil. Reduce heat and simmer, covered. Sauté bacon until fat is rendered. Stir in carrot and onion. Sauté until bacon is browned. Add to soup kettle with the rest of the ingredients. Simmer for 3 hours or until meat falls off the bone. Slice meat into serving pieces and discard bone. Add meat to soup; taste and correct seasonings. Yield: 8 to 10 servings.

Pumpkin Soup

    3 pounds diced, peeled pumpkin
        or 4 cups cooked pumpkin puree
    2 tablespoons margarine or butter
    1 cup sliced onion
    8 green onions, chopped
    6 cups well-seasoned chicken broth
    1 bay leaf
    2 tablespoons margarine
    3 tablespoons flour
    1 cup yogurt
        Freshly ground black pepper
        Salt
        Chopped chives
        Garlic croutons

Pumpkin can be chopped fine in food processor fitted with steel knife, if desired. This will speed up cooking but is not necessary. Sauté onions in margarine in a large soup kettle or Dutch oven until golden. Add pumpkin, broth, and bay leaf. Bring to a boil, reduce heat, and simmer, covered, until pumpkin is soft (10 minutes if using puree). Remove bay leaf. Place mixture in blender and blend until smooth (or strain) and return to Dutch oven. Melt margarine in small saucepan and stir in flour. Cook for about 2 minutes, then add a small amount of soup to flour, stirring constantly. Add more soup; then pour flour mixture into the Dutch oven. Bring soup in Dutch oven to boil; stir with a wire whisk until soup thickens. Taste and correct seasonings. Just before serving, stir in yogurt (or use dollops of yogurt as a garnish). When soup is thoroughly heated (do not boil after yogurt is added), garnish with chives and croutons. Yield: 8 servings.

Quick Spinach or Chard Soup

    3 cups well-flavored beef broth
    3 to 4 cups shredded spinach or chard
        Salt
        Freshly ground black pepper
        Parsley

Bring beef broth to the boiling point; add spinach and reduce heat. Simmer, covered, 5 to 10 minutes or until vegetable is tender. Taste and correct seasonings. Serve garnished with parsley. Yield: 3 to 4 servings.

Oxtail Soup

    2 pounds oxtail, cut into 2-inch pieces
    ¼ cup flour
    1 tablespoon bacon drippings or vegetable oil
    2 cups chopped onion
    5 cups well-seasoned beef, vegetable or
        other stock or water
    5 sprigs parsley
    1 bay leaf
    2 whole cloves
    4 peppercorns
    ½ teaspoon thyme
    ½ teaspoon tarragon
    1 cup carrots, sliced
    2 ribs celery, diced
    1 cup turnips, diced
    1 teaspoon lemon juice
        Salt
        Freshly ground black pepper
    ¾ cup minced parsley

Roll oxtail pieces in flour until lightly coated. Heat oil in a Dutch oven or heavy soup kettle and stir in meat to brown thoroughly. Stir in onions and cook until golden. Pour stock over meat, reduce heat, and add parsley sprigs, bay leaf, cloves, peppercorns, thyme, and tarragon. Cover and simmer about 3 hours. Add vegetables and continue simmering until meat falls from the bones, (1 hour or more). Discard bones, skim fat from the surface, and stir in lemon juice. Taste and correct seasonings; sprinkle on parsley and serve. Yield: 6 to 8 servings.

Note: In a slow cooker, this dish would take about 8 hours on high.

Make broths and stock from the inexpensive bones the butcher has to offer, as well as from the leftover bones from meats and poultry.

Save steaming and cooking liquids from all cooking; freeze if necessary until needed for a highly flavored, nutritious soup.

Save all cooking liquids for later use in flavorful, highly nutritious soups; freeze any liquid which will not be used within a short time.

Cream of Tomato Soup

    2 cups canned tomatoes with juice
    ½ cup chopped onion
    2 ribs celery, chopped
    ¼ cup chopped parsley
      Freshly ground black pepper
    2 tablespoons margarine
    2 tablespoons flour
    3 cups milk
      Salt
      Freshly ground black pepper
      Croutons, parsley, chives, or dollops of yogurt
      to garnish

Cook tomatoes, onion, celery, and parsley together until vegetables are tender. Place in blender and blend until smooth. Meanwhile, stir flour into melted margarine in a heavy saucepan. Cook, stirring regularly, for about 5 minutes over very low heat. Stir in milk gradually, keeping mixture smooth. Stir blended tomato mixture into cream sauce. Taste and correct seasonings. Serve, garnished as desired. Yield: 4 to 6 servings.

The Meiners' Cauliflower Soup

    5 cups cauliflowerets
    2½ cups chicken, onion, or
      vegetable stock
    1 teaspoon soy sauce
    ½ teaspoon paprika
    ½ teaspoon savory
    ½ teaspoon garlic powder
    ¼ teaspoon freshly ground black pepper
    2 teaspoons butter or margarine
    2 teaspoons flour
    1½ cups milk
    ¾ cup nonfat dried milk powder
    ¼ cup freshly grated Parmesan
      or Romano cheese
    ¼ cup grated Swiss cheese
    2 egg yolks, beaten
    3 tablespoons lemon juice

Reserve ½ cup flowerets for garnish. Cook remainder in desired stock with soy sauce, paprika, savory, garlic powder, and black pepper until cauliflower is soft. Puree in blender. Melt butter in a small saucepan; add flour and stir until flour is cooked through. Gradually add milk; cook and stir until thick. Add puree, dried milk, and cheeses. Reheat to melt cheese but do not boil. Beat egg yolks with lemon juice; whisk into ½ cup hot soup and return to remaining soup. Reheat; do not boil. Taste and correct seasonings. Garnish with reserved flowerets and extra cheese, if desired. Yield: 4 to 6 servings.

Winter Garbure (Thick French Stew)

    2 cups Great Northern beans
    8 cups water
    1½ pounds smoked pork rump
      or meaty ham bone
    5 large cloves garlic
    ½ teaspoon thyme
    ½ cup parsley
    ½ teaspoon marjoram
    5 potatoes, peeled and sliced
    2 cups fresh or frozen green beans or peas
    ½ medium-sized green cabbage,
      washed and shredded
      Salt
      Freshly ground black pepper
    8 to 10 slices dry whole wheat bread
    1 cup grated Swiss cheese

Soak beans in water overnight. Bring beans and liquid, pork rump, garlic, and herbs to a boil in a large heavy soup kettle or Dutch oven. Reduce heat and simmer, covered, for 1½ hours. Add potatoes and cook another 30 minutes. Finally, add cabbage and green beans and additional liquid, if needed. Simmer until vegetables are tender. Remove meat to serve separately. Taste and correct seasonings. Ladle soup into ovenproof bowls, placing bread slices on top. Sprinkle Swiss cheese on top and place under broiler until cheese is melted and browned. Serve immediately. Yield: 8 to 10 servings.

Lynn's Budget Chili

    2 cups pinto beans
    6 cups water
    ½ cup chopped onion
    ¼ cup bacon or chicken fat or margarine
    2 cloves garlic, minced
      Cumin to taste
      Chili powder to taste
      Salt to taste
      Freshly ground black pepper to taste
    ½ cup grated sharp Cheddar or Monterey Jack cheese

Soak beans in water overnight. Bring beans, liquid, and onion to a boil. Reduce heat and simmer, covered, for 1 hour. Add more water if necessary. Stir in fat, garlic, cumin, and chili powder. Simmer for 30 minutes. Taste and add salt and pepper. Stir in cheese until it melts. Serve immediately. Yield: 4 to 6 servings.

Danish Apple Soup

- 4 cups quartered apples (unpeeled), cores removed
- 4 cups water
- 1 teaspoon grated lemon rind
- 1 stick cinnamon
- 2 tablespoons cornstarch
- ¼ cup water
- ½ cup dry white wine
- ¼ cup sugar

Place apples, water, lemon rind, and cinnamon in a large, heavy-bottomed saucepan over low heat. Simmer until apples are tender. Remove cinnamon stick and puree mixture in blender (or through sieve) until smooth. For a thinner soup, add more water. Bring mixture to simmer again. Blend cornstarch and water together until smooth. Stir into soup and cook over low heat until soup is thick and smooth. Stir in wine and sugar. Taste and correct seasonings. Serve hot. Yield: 6 servings.

Barley-Vegetable Soup

- 2 tablespoons margarine
- 1 cup chopped onion
- 2 cloves garlic, minced
- 2½ cups well-flavored beef broth or stock
- 6 cups water
- 3 tablespoons tomato paste
  Freshly ground black pepper
- 1 bay leaf
- ½ cup barley
- 2 cups chopped celery and leaves
- 2 cups sliced carrots
- ½ cup chopped parsley
  Salt
  Yogurt

Sauté onions and garlic in margarine until onions are translucent. Add broth, water, tomato paste, pepper, and bay leaf. Heat to boiling. Stir in barley, reduce heat and simmer, covered, 1 hour. Stir in vegetables and simmer, covered, about 30 minutes longer or until vegetables and barley are tender. Taste and correct seasonings. Serve hot, garnished with a dollop of yogurt. Yield: 8 servings.

Add high-protein, low-cost legumes and garden produce to a well-flavored broth for a meal fit for a prince at a price a pauper could afford.

Ham Hock and Bean Soup

- 1 pound Great Northern or navy beans, rinsed and sorted
- 8 cups water
- 4 cups vegetable cooking liquid, broth, or other flavorful liquid on hand
- 1 1-pound smoked ham hock
- 1 cup chopped onion
- 1 cup chopped celery
  Salt
  Freshly ground black pepper

Soak beans overnight in water. Combine soaked beans and liquid with well-flavored broth and ham hock in a large soup kettle or Dutch oven. Bring to boil, reduce heat and simmer, covered, for 2 hours. Add onion and celery and continue to simmer 1 hour. Remove ham hock and slice off meat into bite-sized pieces. Discard bone. Return meat to soup. If desired, mash beans slightly. Taste and correct seasonings. Serve hot. Yield: 6 to 8 servings.

End-of-the-Month Lentil Soup

- 2 slices bacon, chopped
- 1 cup lentils, washed and sorted
- 1 cup carrots, sliced
- 1 cup chopped onion
- 2 ribs celery, chopped
- 3 cloves garlic, minced
- 10 cups stock, vegetable cooking liquid, broth, and/or water
- 1 bay leaf
- ½ cup chopped parsley
- ¼ teaspoon thyme
  Salt
  Freshly ground black pepper

Sauté bacon in a Dutch oven or heavy soup kettle until fat is rendered. Stir in lentils, carrots, onions, celery, and garlic. Sauté for about 5 minutes, stirring regularly. Add remaining ingredients, except salt and pepper, and bring to a boil. Reduce heat and simmer, covered for 1 hour or until lentils and vegetables are tender. Taste and correct seasonings. If desired, put soup through blender. Serve hot. Yield: 8 servings.

Lou Snow's Spanish Lentil Soup

2 tablespoons olive oil
1 green pepper, chopped
¾ cup chopped onion
1 clove garlic, minced
1 heaping tablespoon flour
2 cups stewed or canned tomatoes
1 cup thinly sliced carrots
1 cup dry lentils
1 teaspoon salt
1 quart water
Freshly ground black pepper

Heat oil in a very large frying pan or Dutch oven. Stir in green pepper, onion, and garlic. Cook until soft. Sprinkle with flour, and stir. Add remaining ingredients. Bring to boil; reduce heat and simmer, covered, 2 hours. Taste and correct seasonings. Serve immediately. Yield: 4 to 6 servings.

Soybean and Sausage Stew

2 strips bacon, chopped
1 cup sliced onion
6 carrots, peeled and sliced
3 to 4 cups shredded cabbage
2 cups cooked soybeans
1 tablespoon minced parsley
1 bay leaf
3 to 4 cups water, vegetable stock, or broth
½ pound smoked sausage, cut into serving pieces
Salt
Freshly ground black pepper

Fry bacon in a very large frying pan or Dutch oven until it renders its fat. Stir in onion and sauté until golden. Add carrots, cabbage, soybeans, parsley, bay leaf, and water and simmer, covered, 30 minutes or until vegetables are tender. Stir in sausage and simmer, covered, 15 more minutes. Taste and correct seasonings with salt and pepper. Serve very hot. Yield: 4 to 6 servings.

Corn Chowder

2 tablespoons margarine or butter
1 cup chopped onion
1½ cups peeled and chopped potatoes
4 cups milk
¼ cup non-instant powdered milk
2 cups fresh corn
¼ teaspoon paprika
Freshly ground black pepper
Salt
Parsley, minced

Melt margarine in a Dutch oven or heavy soup kettle. Sauté onion and potatoes in the margarine for about 5 minutes. Add milk which has been mixed with powdered milk, corn, and paprika. Cover and simmer until vegetables are tender. In the last minute of cooking, add salt and pepper to taste. Serve hot, garnished with parsley. Yield: 6 servings.

Zucchini Soup

1 tablespoon margarine
1 cup chopped onion
4 cups well-flavored chicken broth
4 to 6 cups zucchini slices
1 tablespoon fresh dill
Chopped parsley
Unflavored yogurt or sour cream

Melt margarine in a large frying pan or soup kettle. Sauté onion until transparent. Add chicken broth, zucchini, and dill. Simmer 10 to 15 minutes until zucchini is tender. Taste and correct seasonings. Soup can be served as is or placed in a blender until smooth. Garnish with chopped parsley and dollops of yogurt or sour cream, as desired. Yield: 4 to 6 servings.

Julia's Sausage-Vegetable Soup

8 cups water, vegetable cooking liquid, stock, or broth
½ pound sliced Polish, smoked, or other sausage
1 cup sliced carrots
½ cup chopped onion
2 cloves garlic, minced
1 teaspoon marjoram
½ teaspoon thyme
¼ teaspoon freshly ground black pepper
1 bay leaf
1 cup diced potatoes
3 cups thinly sliced cabbage
Salt

In a large soup kettle or Dutch oven, bring water, sausage, carrots, onion, garlic, marjoram, thyme, pepper, and bay leaf to the boiling point. Reduce heat and simmer, covered, 30 minutes. Add potatoes and cabbage and simmer, covered, until vegetables are tender, about 30 minutes. Taste and correct seasonings. Yield: 8 servings.

Fish, Poultry, and Meat

The part of the family food budget that seems to receive more attention than any other is that devoted to fish, poultry, and meat. The important thing to remember is to be flexible—to know that one year you may not be able to afford much bacon, for instance, and another year, not much beef. Try new dishes, including meatless meals, to provide protein without spending a fortune.

Haddock Newburg

1 pound haddock fillets (fresh or frozen)
1½ cups milk
5 tablespoons margarine
¾ cup mushrooms
4 tablespoons unbleached flour
1 egg yolk, lightly beaten
1 teaspoon Worcestershire sauce
1 teaspoon lemon juice
2 tablespoons dry sherry
Salt
Freshly ground black pepper
Chopped parsley

If haddock is frozen, thaw according to package directions. Poach haddock in milk in a large frying pan until fish just begins to flake. Meanwhile, sauté mushrooms in 1 tablespoon margarine until they are lightly browned (8 to 10 minutes). In a small pan, melt remaining margarine. With a wire whisk stir in flour and cook gently for about 2 minutes. When fish is poached, remove from heat and pour the hot milk into the flour mixture. Beat with wire whisk until sauce is thickened. Mix a small amount of the flour-milk mixture with the egg yolk. Gently stir mixture into the cream sauce. Add the seasonings; taste and correct. Finally, stir in the mushrooms and pour the sauce over the fish (break up the fish, if desired). Simmer, stirring constantly, until the dish is heated through, about 2 minutes. Serve over rice, garnished with parsley, if desired. Yield: 3 to 4 servings.

Chinese Beef with Peas and Peanuts

1 10-ounce package frozen peas
   or 1 cup fresh
1 cup vegetable oil
½ cup raw, fresh, unsalted peanuts
1 cup chopped onion
1 small clove garlic, minced
1 cup chopped celery
¾ pound ground beef
1 cup sliced fresh mushrooms, (optional)
1 cup well-flavored beef broth
2 tablespoons cornstarch
2 tablespoons soy sauce
2 tablespoons sherry

Thaw peas slightly. Pour peanuts into hot oil in a wok or large frying pan. Turn off heat and let peanuts stand about 1½ minutes until golden. Drain, leaving 1 tablespoon oil. Stir-fry onion, garlic, and celery and then add ground beef. Cook briskly until just browned. Remove meat and vegetables. Add peas and mushrooms to skillet; pour in broth and cook until peas are crisp-cooked. Mix cornstarch, soy sauce, and sherry; stir into mixture in skillet. Add beef and vegetables and cook, stirring constantly, until sauce thickens. Transfer to serving dish and sprinkle with peanuts. Serve with rice. Yield: 4 to 6 servings.

Roast Stuffed Chicken

1 3- to 4-pound fryer
3 cups slightly dry, cubed bread
1 rib celery, diced
3 tablespoons minced onion
½ teaspoon salt
½ teaspoon crumbled sage
⅛ teaspoon freshly ground black pepper
1 small apple, chopped
¼ cup raisins
2 cloves garlic, minced
2 tablespoons butter or margarine
   at room temperature

Preheat oven to 400°. Wash chicken and pat dry. Mix together remaining ingredients except butter, and stuff chicken. (Any excess can be baked in aluminum foil alongside the bird.) Truss bird as desired and rub skin with butter. Place, breast up, on rack in roasting pan. Roast uncovered 1¾ to 2 hours or until done (drumstick will move up and down easily). Baste occasionally with drippings. Yield: 4 servings.

Hamburger Stroganoff

2 slices bacon, chopped
1 pound ground beef
1 cup chopped onion
2 tablespoons whole wheat flour
2 cups beef broth
¼ pound sliced mushrooms
1 teaspoon Worcestershire sauce
   Salt
   Freshly ground black pepper
1 cup sour cream

Heat bacon in a large frying pan until it begins to render its fat. Stir in ground beef and onion and brown meat thoroughly. Stir in flour and pour in beef broth. Bring to boil, then reduce heat and simmer for about 30 minutes. Stir in mushrooms and Worcestershire sauce and simmer until mushrooms are cooked. Taste and add salt and pepper to taste. Finally, stir in sour cream and heat thoroughly; do not boil. Serve over boiled noodles or rice. Yield: 8 to 10 servings.

Mock Chop Suey

1 tablespoon vegetable oil
1 cup chopped onion
1 cup chopped celery
1 pound ground beef
1 cup uncooked brown rice
1 can cream of mushroom soup
1 can cream of chicken soup
2 tablespoons soy sauce
2 cups bean sprouts (canned sprouts can be used)
1 8-ounce can water chestnuts, drained and sliced (optional)
1 3-ounce can chow mein noodles
1 10-ounce package frozen peas

Preheat oven to 350°. In vegetable oil in a large frying pan, sauté onion and celery for 5 minutes. Add ground beef and brown well. Stir in rice and cook until transparent. Finally, stir in soups, soy sauce, bean sprouts, and water chestnuts. Bake in a large casserole, uncovered for 30 minutes. Stir in ⅓ can chow mein noodles and frozen peas. (Add water if mixture is too dry.) Bake 30 more minutes or until rice is just tender; sprinkle remaining noodles on top and bake 10 minutes more. Serve immediately. Can be frozen before baking. Thaw and bake, following directions for adding noodles and peas. Yield: 10 servings.

The Benvenutos' Pizza

½ package active dry yeast
¾ cup lukewarm water
1 cup whole wheat flour
1 cup unbleached flour
   Olive oil

Sprinkle yeast into water; stir until dissolved. Add 1 cup of whole wheat flour and stir thoroughly. Add 1 cup unbleached flour; continue to stir until dough can be turned out onto a lightly floured board. Knead 10 minutes or until dough is pliable. Oil a bowl with olive oil, place dough into the bowl and turn to grease all surfaces. Cover and put in a warm place (85°); let rise until doubled in bulk (about 1½ hours). Oil an 11 x 17 x 1-inch baking sheet with olive oil; with greased hands, spread dough in pan. Brush olive oil evenly on top of crust to keep topping from sinking in. Spread on the topping and bake in a 425° oven for 25 to 30 minutes or until done. Yield: 12 slices pizza.

Topping

2 cups Grandma Ben's Tomato Sauce (page 47)
1 pound mozzarella cheese, sliced thin
1 green pepper, diced
   Thin slices pepperoni, chopped, shaved ham,
   or 1 2-ounce can anchovies
2 tablespoons oregano

Spread tomato sauce on pizza crust; cover with cheese; add green pepper and other desired topping. Finally, sprinkle oregano over all.

Scalloped Potatoes and Ham

2 tablespoons margarine
2 tablespoons whole wheat flour
2 cups milk
1½ pounds potatoes, sliced thin (4 medium-sized)
¾ pound ham, sliced into bite-sized pieces

Preheat oven to 350°. Melt margarine in a small, heavy-bottomed saucepan. Stir in flour and cook for a few minutes until golden. Add milk and stir with wire whisk until sauce is thickened. Remove from heat. Pour a small amount of the sauce into the bottom of a greased, 2-quart casserole. Layer potatoes, ham, and white sauce into casserole, finishing with white sauce. Cover and bake for about 1¼ hours. Remove cover and bake 15 more minutes or until potatoes are tender. Yield: 4 servings.

Easy, Cheesy Fish Fillets

2 pounds cod, halibut, flounder or
  other white fish fillets
1 tablespoon lemon juice
⅛ teaspoon thyme
  Salt
  Freshly ground black pepper
⅓ cup finely grated bread crumbs
1¼ cups grated Swiss cheese
2 tablespoons margarine or butter

If fish is frozen, thaw at room temperature until fillets will separate. Rinse lightly and pat dry with paper towels. Preheat oven to 350° and lightly grease a baking dish that will hold all the fillets in one layer. Arrange fillets in dish, sprinkle with lemon juice, thyme, and salt and pepper to taste. Bake for 25 minutes or until fish begins to look opaque. Mix together the crumbs and cheese; remove dish from oven and sprinkle cheese mixture over the top evenly. Dot with margarine and return to oven for another 10 minutes or until fish flakes easily with a fork. Yield: 4 to 6 servings.

For high-quality, no-waste meals which can be relatively inexpensive, watch for fish specials. Sniff the package of frozen fish; if it smells "fishy," don't buy it.

Stuffed Cabbage

1 medium-size Savoy cabbage, chilled
½ pound pork sausage
1 cup chopped onion
3 cups meaty broth
  Freshly ground black pepper
  Salt

Steam cabbage until just pliable. Brown pork sausage with chopped onion until pork is well cooked. When cabbage is steamed, chop the core into small pieces and stir into pork mixture. Cook a few minutes to blend well. Taste and correct seasonings. Place cabbage stem down, on a piece of cheesecloth large enough to tie around the cabbage. Place pork mixture among the leaves and reshape cabbage. Bring cheesecloth up around cabbage and tie on top so that cabbage holds its shape. Place in a pot over meaty broth and simmer, covered, for about 1 hour or until cabbage is tender. Remove cheesecloth before serving. You can reserve broth for another purpose or serve as a soup for the first course. Taste and correct seasonings before serving. Yield: 4 servings.

Lemon Chicken

4 large chicken breasts, split in half
¼ cup margarine or butter, melted
½ cup whole wheat flour
2 tablespoons olive or vegetable oil
1½ cups sliced onion
3 cloves garlic, minced
1 tablespoon crumbled, dried oregano
  Juice of 1 lemon
  Freshly ground black pepper
½ teaspoon salt

Wash chicken breasts and pat dry with towels. Spread butter on all sides of the chicken; then roll breasts in flour. Over medium heat in a large skillet or Dutch oven, heat the oil. Stir in onion and garlic and cook until golden. Add chicken and cook, turning occasionally, for 20 minutes. Add remaining ingredients and cook, covered, for 15 to 20 minutes, or until chicken is tender. Taste and correct seasonings before serving. Serve with buttered pasta, Fettucine Alfredo, or Risotto. Yield: 8 servings.

Risotto

1 tablespoon margarine
1 cup chopped onion
1 cup rice
2½ cups chicken broth
  Salt
  Freshly ground black pepper

Heat margarine over medium heat until melted; stir in onion and cook until translucent. Add rice and cook until the rice is coated with butter. Stir in broth and simmer, covered, until the liquid is absorbed and the rice is tender. If additional liquid is needed, add more broth or a small amount of white wine. Taste and correct seasonings before serving. Yield: 4 servings.

Rather than buy sliced ham for sandwiches, check the regular hams or picnics and after cooking, slice them. Freeze what won't be used immediately for casseroles, soups, and other uses. To eliminate the saltiness of ham, boil the meat in several changes of water; much of the saltiness will boil out.

Fish, Poultry and Meat

Creole Stuffed Peppers

    3 very large (or 6 small) green stuffing peppers
    ½ pound ground beef
    ¼ cup chopped onion
    2 cups cooked rice
    ½ teaspoon salt
      Freshly ground black pepper
    1 tablespoon vegetable oil
    ⅓ cup diced celery
    2 cloves garlic, minced
    2 cups seasoned tomato sauce plus 1 cup water
      or 3 cups tomatoes in juice
    1 teaspoon Worcestershire sauce
    ⅛ teaspoon ground cloves
    2 tablespoons minced parsley
      Salt
      Freshly ground black pepper
    1 to 2 cups whole kernel corn

Remove core, membrane, and seeds from peppers. Sauté ground beef and ¼ cup onion (adding oil only if necessary) until meat is browned. Remove from heat and stir in rice, salt, and pepper. In a medium-sized skillet, sauté remaining onion, celery, and garlic in oil until onion is translucent. Stir in tomato sauce and remaining seasonings. Taste and correct. Stir ¼ cup sauce into rice mixture. Stuff peppers with rice mixture. Place peppers in slow-cooker, pour remainder of sauce around them, and cook 6 to 8 hours on low or 3 hours on high. Add corn, if desired, in the last 1 to 2 hours of cooking. Yield: 3 to 6 servings.

Note: To decrease cooking time, steam pepper cases and continue with the recipe from that point, baking peppers in sauce at 350° for 30 minutes or until tender.

Perfect Scrod

    1 pound scrod fillets (thawed, if frozen) or
      other similar fish
    ½ cup milk
    ½ cup bread crumbs
    1 tablespoon margarine or butter
      Lemon wedges

Preheat oven to 350°. Place fillets in a 2-quart casserole. Pour milk over and bake for 10 to 12 minutes or until fillets are white. Pour off milk. Sprinkle bread crumbs on top of fish, dot with butter, and broil 3 to 4 minutes until crumbs become crisp. Serve immediately. Yield: 2 to 3 servings.

Easy Curried Cod Fillets

    1 pound frozen cod fillets, thawed
    ¼ teaspoon salt
    2 tablespoons margarine
    1½ teaspoons curry powder
    1 cup chopped onion
    1 cup chopped apples

Preheat oven to 350°. Place fillets in a well-greased baking dish. Sprinkle with salt. Melt margarine in frying pan; stir in curry powder, onion, and apples. Cook for about 5 minutes. Pour onion mixture onto fillets. Cover baking dish with foil, and bake for 30 minutes or until fish flakes easily with fork. Remove foil near the end of baking time to allow fish to brown slightly. Yield: 4 servings.

Meatball Stew

    1 pound ground beef
    ½ cup bread crumbs
    ¼ cup minced onion
    4 tablespoons minced parsley
    1 teaspoon salt
    ¼ teaspoon freshly ground black pepper
    ½ teaspoon crushed oregano
    ¼ teaspoon crushed sweet basil
    1 egg
    ¼ cup milk
    2 tablespoons vegetable oil
    1 green pepper, cut into strips
    4 cups cooked or canned red kidney beans
    3 to 4 cups canned tomatoes
    2 cups tomato sauce (16 ounces)
    1 bay leaf
    ½ teaspoon crushed oregano
    ⅓ teaspoon crushed basil
    1 teaspoon fennel seed, optional
      Shredded cheese

Combine first 10 ingredients in a bowl. Mix lightly, but thoroughly. Shape into 30 meatballs. Heat vegetable oil in a large frying pan or Dutch oven; brown half the meatballs. Remove and drain. Pour off all but 2 tablespoons of pan drippings and sauté green pepper strips until tender. Stir in remaining ingredients, mixing well. Add meatballs. Bring mixture to the boil; reduce heat, cover, and simmer 30 minutes, stirring occasionally. Taste and correct seasonings. Serve in soup bowls, garnished with shredded cheese. Yield: 10 servings.

Alpine Casserole

- 2 pounds (or more) boneless pork shoulder butt (smoked)—also called a cottage ham
- 2 cups sliced onion
- 4 large cloves garlic, minced
- 3 tablespoons whole wheat flour
  Freshly ground black pepper
- ¾ teaspoon dried sweet basil
- 2 tablespoons chopped parsley
- ⅛ teaspoon nutmeg
- 6 large potatoes, peeled and sliced
- 1½ pounds fresh or frozen green beans, trimmed and halved

Trim excess surface fat from shoulder butt. Cover with water in a saucepan. Simmer, covered, 1½ to 2 hours, until meat is tender. Reserve broth. In a very large kettle or Dutch oven, heat oil over medium heat and cook onion and garlic until they are golden. Stir in flour thoroughly and cook a few minutes, stirring constantly. Gradually pour 3 cups of the pork broth into the onion mixture, stirring constantly until sauce is smooth. Add seasonings; put the meat in the center of the Dutch oven and surround with potato slices and green beans. Simmer over low heat, covered, for about 1 hour or until the vegetables are tender. (Occasionally stir vegetables and turn meat during cooking.) Taste and correct seasonings before serving. Yield: 8 servings.

Carolyn's Sicilian Pasta

- 6 quarts water
- 1 cup chopped onion
- 1 tablespoon olive oil
- 2 cloves garlic, minced
- 3 3¾-ounce cans sardines in oil, drained and mashed
- 1 2-ounce can anchovies, drained and mashed, optional
- 1 tablespoon fennel seed
- ¼ cup raisins
- 1 tablespoon chopped parsley
  Freshly ground black pepper
- 1½ pounds spaghetti, fettuccini, or other pasta

In a large kettle, bring water to a boil. In a skillet sauté onion in oil until tender. Stir in remaining ingredients, except spaghetti, in order and cook over low heat until heated through. When water boils, stir in spaghetti. Cook until "al dente." Serve immediately with sauce. Yield: 6 servings.

Note: This recipe is ideal for the cook in a hurry. The pasta should be cooked by the time the sauce is ready.

Beefy Yorkshire Pudding

- 1 pound ground beef
- ½ cup chopped onion
- ¾ teaspoon salt
  Freshly ground black pepper
- 2 sprigs parsley, minced
- 3 eggs
- 1½ cups milk
- 1½ cups unbleached flour
- ¼ teaspoon salt
- ½ teaspoon Worcestershire sauce

Preheat oven to 400°. Brown ground beef and onion in a skillet until onion is tender. Drain off fat; pour ⅓ cup of the drippings into the bottom of a 10 x 13-inch baking pan. Add salt, pepper, and parsley to ground beef mixture. Beat eggs until foamy; add remaining ingredients and beat until smooth. Pour half the egg batter into the bottom of the baking pan. Spoon meat mixture evenly over batter. Pour remaining batter on top. Bake 30 to 35 minutes or until golden. Yield: 6 servings.

Diana Johnson's Chicken Enchiladas

- 1 chicken, cooked, deboned and diced
- 1 tablespoon vegetable oil
- ½ cup chopped onion
- 1 clove garlic, minced
- 5 small whole green chilies, canned or fresh, chopped (more or less to taste)
- 1 cup tomato sauce (8 ounces)
- 3 cups (24 ounces) canned tomatoes
  Salt
  Freshly ground black pepper
- 12 to 15 corn tortillas
- 2 tablespoons vegetable oil, heated
- 1 pound Monterey Jack cheese, grated
- 1 to 2 cups sour cream, optional

Heat vegetable oil in a large frying pan. Sauté onion and garlic in oil until onion begins to soften. Stir in chilies, tomato sauce, and canned tomatoes. Simmer 5 minutes. Add diced chicken, salt and pepper to taste. Simmer 20 minutes. Preheat oven to 350°. Dip tortillas into hot vegetable oil quickly, just to soften tortilla. Divide chicken mixture among tortillas and roll. Place in a large, lightly greased flat baking dish and top with cheese. Bake until cheese melts and enchiladas are hot, 15 to 20 minutes. Top with sour cream, if desired. Yield: 12 to 15 servings.

Meatless Main Dishes

While much of the protein in our diet comes from meat, it is possible to obtain sufficient protein even from meatless meals using protein "complements." Since not all grains and legumes have complete proteins within themselves, eating foods from the following complementary groups will ensure more than adequate protein intake: whole grains and milk products; legumes and seeds; rice and beans; whole grains and legumes.

Split Pea Croquettes

    1 cup split peas
2½ cups boiling water
    2 tablespoons butter or margarine
      Freshly grated nutmeg
    2 tablespoons minced onion
    1 egg, beaten
    1 slice whole wheat bread broken
      into soft crumbs
½ cup raw wheat germ

Gradually drop split peas into boiling water, making certain water continues to boil. Reduce heat, cover, and simmer 25 minutes or until peas are tender. Preheat oven to 350°. Drain (reserving liquid) and place peas in blender or a sieve. Puree and add butter, nutmeg, onion, egg, and bread crumbs. If the mixture won't hold together, add a little of the reserved cooking liquid. Form into oblong patties and roll in wheat germ. Chill if necessary. Place on well greased baking sheet and bake for about 5 minutes; turn and bake another 5 minutes or until lightly-browned. Croquettes may also be fried until browned. Yield: 6 servings.

Banana-Tofu-Peanut Butter Sandwiches

    8 slices whole wheat bread
    1 banana
    1 teaspoon lemon juice
    1 cup tofu
½ cup peanut butter

Mash banana thoroughly; mix in lemon juice. Mash tofu; blend in tofu and peanut butter until thoroughly mixed. Spread on bread and garnish as desired. Yield: approximately 8 open-faced sandwiches.

If desired, garnish with strawberry halves, pineapple slices, orange slices, mandarin orange segments, chopped nuts, raisins, cinnamon, etc.

Julia's Black Beans and Rice with Tomato Sauce

2½ cups dried black beans
    7 cups water, broth, or vegetable cooking liquid
¼ teaspoon freshly ground black pepper
    3 garlic cloves, minced
    1 large onion, peeled, studded with 4 whole cloves
    2 tablespoons vegetable oil
    1 large green pepper, seeded and chopped
    1 cup chopped onion
      Salt

Bring beans and water to a boil in a large, heavy saucepan or Dutch oven. Boil for 2 minutes, remove from heat, cover, and let stand for at least 1 hour. Add black pepper to beans and reheat; cover and simmer for 1 hour. Stir garlic and whole onion into beans; simmer, covered, 30 minutes longer or until beans are tender. Heat oil in a medium-size frying pan; stir in pepper and onion. Sauté until onions are golden. Remove whole onion from beans, and, if desired, chop onion and return to beans along with sautéed pepper and onion mixture. Add salt to taste; correct seasonings. Serve over rice with Tomato Sauce. Yield: 8 servings.

Tomato Sauce

    2 cups canned tomatoes, drained
¾ cup chopped sweet onion
    2 cloves garlic, minced
    1 teaspoon vegetable oil
    1 tablespoon wine vinegar
    1 tablespoon parsley, minced
      Dash bottled hot pepper sauce

Place ingredients into blender container and blend until smooth. Refrigerate sauce overnight to allow flavors to combine. Serve with Julia's Black Beans and Rice.

Meatless foods which have complete proteins are soybeans and soy products, cottonseed flour, eggs, nutritional (brewers') yeast, wheat germ, and milk and milk products such as nonfat milk and cheese. Several of these offer very inexpensive sources of protein.

Spinach-Onion Stuffed Crepes

　3　pounds spinach and/or Swiss chard
　2　cups minced onion
　4　tablespoons margarine
2½　tablespoons flour
　¾　cup milk
　1　cup grated Swiss cheese
　　　Salt
　　　Freshly ground black pepper
20　crepes

Wash spinach thoroughly and steam until tender (about 10 minutes). Press excess liquid out and place spinach in a grinder fitted with a fine blade. Meanwhile, sauté onion in margarine until tender. Stir in cooked and minced spinach until well blended. Add flour and cook again. Stir in milk and cook until sauce is thickened. Finally add cheese and season to taste. Divide spinach among crepes; roll up and place in a well-greased baking dish. Cover with foil. Bake immediately at 350° for 30 minutes or refrigerate and bake as needed for 40 minutes.

Batter for Crepes

　1　cup whole wheat flour
　1　cup unbleached flour
　½　teaspoon salt
　4　eggs, lightly beaten
　2　cups milk
　7　tablespoons vegetable oil

Mix flour and salt together in a medium-sized bowl. Make a well in the middle and pour in eggs. Beat until smooth. Add milk slowly, keeping batter smooth. Finally, add oil. Let rest several hours. Stir well just before using and pour by the ladleful into a lightly greased, 9-inch crepe pan. Turn when first side is golden and cook other side. Repeat until all batter is used. Set crepes aside on paper towels until ready for filling, or keep hot if using immediately.

Chris's Cottage Cheese Pancakes

　1　cup cottage cheese
　3　eggs
　¼　cup raw wheat germ
　¼　cup unbleached or whole wheat flour
　1　teaspoon vanilla

Beat cottage cheese and eggs together thoroughly. Stir in wheat germ, flour, and vanilla lightly. Cook on very hot griddle; when well browned on one side, flip and brown the other. Yield: 1 dozen pancakes.

Stuffed Eggplant

　2　tablespoons vegetable or olive oil
　2　cups chopped onion
　2　cloves garlic, minced
　½　cup chopped carrot
　1　cup chopped celery
　½　cup chopped parsley
　4　fresh mint leaves (or 1 teaspoon dried)
　1　cup canned tomatoes, with juice
　1　teaspoon salt
　¼　teaspoon freshly ground black pepper
　1　eggplant (weighing about 2 pounds)
　½　cup cooked brown rice

In a large frying pan, cook onion in oil until translucent. Stir in all ingredients except eggplant and rice. Simmer for about 30 minutes. Cut eggplant lengthwise, scoop out pulp, leaving a ⅜-inch shell. Chop pulp and cook with vegetables until tender. Add a teaspoon of tomato juice, if necessary. Preheat oven to 350°. Stir in rice and stuff mixture into eggplant. Place eggplant halves in a well-greased casserole. Cover tightly and bake about 1½ hours or until tender. Yield: 6 servings.

Vic's Kidney Bean Casserole

　¼　cup butter or margarine
1½　cups sliced onion
　2　large cloves garlic, minced
　1　medium green pepper, seeded and chopped
　4　cups cooked, red kidney beans (drained)
　⅓　teaspoon ground cloves
　3　tablespoons tomato puree or paste
　1　cup dry red wine
　　　Salt
　　　Freshly ground black pepper

Melt butter in a large frying pan; stir in onion, garlic, and green pepper. Cook until onion is transparent. Preheat oven to 375°. Mix beans, onion mixture, cloves, puree, and wine in a large casserole dish. Taste and season with salt and pepper, as desired. Bake for about 45 minutes or until mixture is hot and bubbly. Yield: 6 servings.

Mom's Zucchini Pancakes

4 medium zucchini, grated
½ cup grated onion
3 eggs, beaten
1 teaspoon salt
½ cup raw wheat germ

Mix ingredients together thoroughly. Drop by tablespoonsful onto a lightly greased griddle. Brown on both sides. Serve with yogurt or apple-sauce. Yield: 4 servings.

Irene's Cheese and Spinach Pie

1 tablespoon margarine or vegetable oil
¼ pound sliced mushrooms
1 small zucchini, thinly sliced
1 green pepper, diced
1 cup diced ham
1 pound drained ricotta or cottage cheese
1 cup grated mozzarella
3 eggs, lightly beaten
½ cup cooked, drained, and chopped spinach
1 tablespoon diced dill
    Salt
    Freshly ground black pepper
1 tablespoon melted butter or margarine

Sauté mushrooms, zucchini, and green pepper in margarine for 5 minutes or until vegetables are soft. Add ham and sauté 2 minutes more or until all moisture is evaporated. Cool. Preheat oven to 350°. Combine cottage cheese with mozzarella, eggs, and spinach. Finally, beat in ham mixture and dill. Season to taste. Pour mixture into an oiled pie plate or casserole dish which will hold about 1½ quarts. Sprinkle with melted butter and bake 45 minutes or until set. Yield: 6 to 8 servings.

Eggplant Creole

1 tablespoon vegetable oil
1 cup chopped onion
½ cup chopped celery
2 cups eggplant, cut into 1-inch cubes
½ cup chopped green pepper
1 cup tomato sauce
1 bay leaf
    Salt
    Cayenne pepper

Sauté onion in oil until onion is translucent; stir in remaining ingredients, except salt and pepper, in order. Cover and simmer until eggplant is tender. Taste and add salt and cayenne to taste. Yield: 4 servings.

Soybean Loaf

1 cup dry, cooking soybeans, washed and sorted
2 cups water
½ cup well-flavored broth or vegetable cooking liquid
1 tablespoon vegetable oil
½ cup chopped onion
1 clove garlic, minced
⅛ teaspoon sage
1 cup bread crumbs
1 cup canned tomatoes, well chopped
    Salt
    Freshly ground black pepper
2 eggs, beaten

Soak beans for about 2 hours in the 2 cups water. Place container in freezer and freeze until solid. Bring vegetable cooking liquid to a boil and drop the frozen soybeans into it. Cover and simmer 2 to 4 hours or until soybeans are tender. Grind soybeans very fine in a food grinder. Preheat oven to 350°. Sauté onion in oil until golden. Stir in garlic, sage, bread crumbs, tomatoes, and cooked soybeans. Taste and correct seasonings. Finally, add beaten eggs. Pour into a well-greased 8½ x 4½ x 1-inch loaf pan. Bake 45 minutes or until done. Serve as is or with a tomato sauce. Yield: 6 servings.

Fettuccine Alfredo

1 pound noodles
3 quarts rapidly boiling, salted water
1 cup margarine, melted
2 cups freshly grated Romano or Parmesan cheese
⅓ cup milk
¼ cup powdered milk
    Freshly ground black pepper
    Minced parsley (optional)

Cook noodles in water until tender. Drain and place in a large serving dish that can be heated on low burner. Then slowly add cheese. Mix milk and powdered milk together and stir into noodles gently. When well blended, stir in pepper, to taste, and minced parsley, if desired. Yield: 6 servings.

Chinese Walnut Tofu Dinner

    1 cup broken walnuts
    3 tablespoons vegetable oil
    1 cup sliced onion
1½ cups celery, sliced lengthwise
    1 cup sliced mushrooms
1¼ cups vegetable broth
    1 tablespoon cornstarch
    2 tablespoons soy sauce
    2 tablespoons dry sherry
    1 cup tofu, cut into small cubes
    1 10-ounce package tiny green peas
      (fresh or frozen)
    1 5-ounce can bamboo shoots, drained
    1 5-ounce can water chestnuts, drained and
      sliced

Toast walnuts in hot vegetable oil in a large frying pan or wok. Remove walnuts and drain on paper towels. Stir in onion, celery, and mushrooms. Stir-fry until onion is tender. Mix together the vegetable broth, cornstarch, soy sauce, and sherry. Pour into wok. Stir until sauce thickens. Stir in tofu, green peas, bamboo shoots, and water chestnuts. Heat thoroughly. When peas are just tender, sprinkle walnuts on top and serve immediately with Brown Rice. Yield: 4 to 6 servings.

Brown Rice

3½ cups water
1½ cups brown rice
    1 tablespoon margarine
    1 teaspoon salt
    1 bay leaf
    1 tablespoon parsley, optional
    ¼ teaspoon thyme
      Freshly ground black pepper

Bring water to boil, stir in rest of ingredients, reduce heat and simmer, covered, until all water is absorbed. Fluff rice with fork before serving. Yield: 8 servings.

Even a child's peanut butter sandwich made with whole grain bread and non-hydrogenated peanut butter contains the complementary proteins of whole grains and legumes. Add a glass of milk, carrot sticks and an apple to create an inexpensive, nutritious lunch that children will actually eat.

Olive-Nut Sandwiches with Alfalfa Sprouts

    8 thin slices whole wheat bread
    1 3-ounce package cream cheese, softened
    2 tablespoons toasted wheat germ
    ¼ cup chopped walnuts
    8 to 10 pimiento-stuffed olives, chopped
    1 cup alfalfa sprouts, firmly packed

Cream together cheese, wheat germ, and nuts until well blended. Stir in olives. Spread mixture on all the bread slices. Divide alfalfa sprouts among four slices. Assemble sandwiches. Yield: 4 sandwiches.

Note: Can also be used on open-faced sandwiches or on small rounds as hors d'oeuvres; or form into a cheese ball, roll in wheat germ, and served as a cracker spread.

Chris's Bhanoo Rice

2½ tablespoons butter
    5 cups rice
    1 teaspoon turmeric
    ¼ teaspoon cardamom
   10 cups water
      Stir-fried vegetables and nuts, (cauliflower, peas, carrots, peanuts, etc.)
      Salt
      Freshly ground black pepper

Melt butter in a large skillet or Dutch oven. Stir in rice and seasonings and cook, stirring constantly, for 5 to 8 minutes or until rice is golden. Add water and cover. Reduce heat to low and cook until all water is absorbed (10 to 20 minutes). Mix in choice of stir-fried vegetables and nuts. Re-fry for several minutes at low heat. Add salt and pepper to taste and serve. Yield: 10 servings.

Parslied Rice

2½ cups uncooked rice
    2 tablespoons margarine
    5 cups vegetable broth
      Salt
      Freshly ground black pepper
    ½ cup finely chopped parsley

Combine rice, margarine, and broth in a large, heavy saucepan. Heat to boiling, stir well, and cover. Reduce heat and simmer 30 minutes or until rice is tender. (Add more broth if necessary.) Taste and add salt and pepper, if necessary. Fold in parsley and serve immediately. Yield: 8 servings.

Salads and Vegetables

For some reason, Americans are paying less attention to vegetables than ever before. Yet vegetables are an important part of our diet. Often, adding a second or third vegetable to a meal supplies high nutrition at a modest cost. Put a garden plot (rent or borrow one, if necessary) to work. Even in a northern climate, it's possible to have huge, green, nourishing salads in mid to late May—just about the time that many people are just beginning to think about planting a garden.

Navy Bean Salad

    2 cups dry navy beans
    2 to 3 tablespoons chopped chives
    5 green onions, with tops, chopped
    5 tablespoons finely chopped parsley
    3 tablespoons olive or vegetable oil
    2 tablespoons lemon juice
    1 tablespoon wine vinegar
    1 tablespoon soy sauce, optional
       Salt
       Freshly ground black pepper
    1 cup sliced radishes, garnish

Wash and sort navy beans. Soak in enough water to cover overnight. Heat to boiling, then reduce heat; simmer until tender (about 1½ hours). Cool. Drain. Mix vegetables with cooled beans. Combine the liquid ingredients in a covered jar or blender and blend well. Pour dressing over salad and marinate overnight. Taste and add salt and pepper; correct other seasonings, if necessary. Garnish with radishes. Yield: 8 servings.

Mom's Sauerkraut Salad

    2 cups packed down sauerkraut,
       drained and chopped (if desired)
    1 cup chopped celery
    ½ cup chopped onion
    1 small green pepper, chopped
    1 teaspoon caraway seeds (or more, to taste)
    ¼ teaspoon fresh horseradish, optional
       Pimiento, optional

Mix ingredients well and let stand 24 hours. (Add a little of the drained juice for a less dry salad.) Serve cold with chopped pimiento for color. Yield: 4 to 6 servings.

Remember that the darker green, leafy vegetables are generally highest in nutrition, yet often lowest in cost.

Marinated Green Beans

    2 pounds green beans
    ½ cup vegetable oil
    3 tablespoons wine vinegar
    ¾ teaspoon salt
       Freshly ground black pepper
    1 teaspoon French mustard
    1 to 2 cloves garlic, minced
       Parsley, minced

Cut the tips and tails off well-washed green beans. Steam until just tender. Reserve steaming liquid for soup or other purpose. Set beans aside to cool quickly. Meanwhile, mix the rest of the ingredients together in a blender or shake vigorously in a covered jar. Pour over cooled beans and toss gently. Cover and refrigerate for at least 2 hours before serving, tossing gently from time to time. Garnish with minced parsley. Yield: 10 servings.

Steamed Celery

    3 cups celery, sliced
       Celery seed
       Salt
       Freshly ground black pepper
       Toasted sunflower seeds

In a vegetable steamer, steam celery until just tender. Season to taste with seeds, salt, and pepper. Sprinkle sunflower seeds over all and serve hot. Yield: 4 servings.

Main Dish Salad

    6 cups shredded greens
       Salt
       Freshly ground black pepper
    5 hard-cooked eggs, shelled and sliced thin
    1 10-ounce package frozen peas
    2 cups shredded Swiss cheese
    ½ cup bacon bits, crisp-cooked, drained, and crumbled
    1 cup salad dressing or mayonnaise
    ¼ cup sliced green onion with tops
       Paprika

Place half the greens into a large salad bowl. Sprinkle with salt and pepper. Layer eggs on top of greens and sprinkle again with salt and pepper. Place remaining greens on top, then add peas, cheese, and bacon bits in order. Spread mayonnaise evenly over top. Cover well and chill about 24 hours. Toss well before serving. Garnish with green onion and paprika. Yield: 12 servings.

Salads and Vegetables

Bavarian Cabbage

4 strips bacon, diced
1 tablespoon brown sugar
½ cup chopped onion
½ cup chopped apple
2 pounds green cabbage, chopped or shredded
   Caraway seed, to taste
1 cup beef or other stock
3 tablespoons dry white wine
2 tablespoons cider or wine vinegar, to taste
   Salt
   Freshly ground black pepper

In a very large frying pan over medium heat, brown bacon. Add sugar and stir until melted. Add onion and apple and simmer a few minutes. Stir in cabbage and caraway seeds thoroughly; pour in stock. Cover and simmer 1 to 1½ hours. Just before serving, stir in wine and vinegar to taste. Add salt and pepper as desired. Yield: 6 to 8 servings.

Note: Can be simmered in casserole in oven if something else is baking.

Marinated Carrot Salad

2 pounds carrots, scrubbed and sliced
   into 1-inch lengths
¾ teaspoon salt
   Freshly ground black pepper
1 teaspoon prepared French mustard
½ cup vegetable oil
½ cup cider vinegar
1 cup tomato sauce
1 cup onion, minced
1 cup green pepper, minced
   Parsley

Steam carrots until just tender (about 10 minutes); cool. Place salt, pepper, and mustard into a medium-size bowl. Beat in a small amount of oil to blend with seasonings. Add remaining oil, beating continuously; finally add vinegar and tomato sauce. Stir in onion and green pepper and taste; correct seasonings. Lightly fold carrots into vinegar and oil mixture, cover tightly, and chill for at least 8 hours or overnight. Serve alone or on salad greens, garnished with parsley. Yield: 10 to 12 servings.

Continue an herb garden through the winter by planting or transplanting herbs into pots. Basil, mint, parsley, coriander, chives, oregano, and others do well indoors but need plenty of light.

Stir-fried Cauliflower

1 tablespoon vegetable oil
⅓ cup sliced or slivered almonds
1 tablespoon butter or margarine
1 medium-large cauliflower, broken into flowerets
½ cup water
   Freshly ground black pepper
1 tablespoon cornstarch
1 tablespoon water
   Salt

Heat oil in a wok or large frying pan. Stir in almonds until they are golden. Remove to absorbent paper. Add butter and flowerets and stir over medium heat for about 3 minutes. Add ½ cup water and pepper to taste; cover and simmer 5 minutes. Mix cornstarch with remaining water; pour into wok and stir gently until sauce thickens. Cauliflower should be tender-crisp. Serve immediately, sprinkled with toasted almonds. Yield: 4 to 6 servings.

Diana's Winter Salad

2 to 3 cups chopped cabbage
2 carrots, chopped
½ tomato, chopped
½ green pepper, chopped
   Creamy dressing, such as Thousand Island, French, blue cheese
   Mayonnaise
   Prepared mustard, optional

Mix vegetables in a serving bowl. Combine creamy dressing and mayonnaise, to taste and in quantity desired. Add mustard to taste. Pour over salad and toss gently but thoroughly. Chill, if desired, before serving. Yield: 4 to 6 servings.

Hot Pepper and Celery Sambal

3 to 4 short or long green chilies (shorter ones are usually hotter)
1 sweet or hot red pepper, chopped fine
1 cup finely chopped celery
1 tablespoon lemon or lime juice
¼ teaspoon shrimp paste (trassi) or anchovy paste, optional

Wash chilies and cut off stems. Cut open and remove seeds, taking care that chilies or juice do not touch face or eyes (or they will burn). Chop chilies fine and wash hands thoroughly after handling. Combine chopped chilies, pepper, celery, and lemon juice together and refrigerate until needed. Serve with curried dishes. Guests can help themselves to make their curries as hot as desired. Yield: approximately 2 cups.

Indonesian Fruit Salad

    1 15-ounce can pineapple chunks, drained
    2 tablespoons brown sugar
    2 tablespoons lemon juice
    2 cups apples, quartered and sliced
    2 tablespoons lemon juice
    1 large pear, quartered and sliced
    1 orange, segmented
    1 cup raw sweet potato, pared and sliced
    2 cups quartered and sliced cucumber
    1 ripe avocado, peeled and cut into strips

Pour drained pineapple juice into a small pan; add sugar and lemon juice. Heat until sugar is dissolved. Cool. Sprinkle lemon juice over apples and avocados to keep slices from turning brown. Place fruits and vegetables in a large salad bowl. Pour cooled pineapple sauce over salad ingredients and toss carefully. Cover the salad bowl with plastic wrap and chill salad until serving time. Yield: 8 servings.

Indonesian Vegetable Salad

    2 cups sliced red onion
    2 cups thinly sliced cucumber
    2 cups shredded carrot
    6 cups thinly sliced cabbage
    ½ cup white vinegar
    ¼ cup vegetable oil
    ½ cup cold water
    1 tablespoon grated fresh ginger
    1 to 2 tablespoons brown sugar
    1½ teaspoons salt

Place vegetables in a large salad bowl. Mix together vinegar, oil, water, ginger, sugar, and salt. Pour over cabbage mixture and stir lightly. Refrigerate at least 3 to 4 hours before serving, stirring every hour or so. Yield: 8 to 10 servings.

Classic Vinegar and Oil Dressing

    ⅔ cup vegetable or olive oil
    ⅓ cup red wine vinegar (or part lemon juice)
    ¼ teaspoon salt
      Freshly ground black pepper
    1 tablespoon minced chives
    1 tablespoon minced parsley
    ½ teaspoon dry mustard
    1 clove garlic, minced, optional
      Any other fresh herbs desired, minced

Place all the above ingredients in a jar, cover tightly, and shake. Taste and correct seasonings. Chill until needed, shaking just before using. Yield: 1 cup.

Moroccan Carrot Salad

    1 pound carrots, scraped
    ¼ cup vegetable or olive oil
    3 tablespoons lemon juice
    1 large clove garlic, minced
    ½ teaspoon cumin
    ½ teaspoon dried mint leaves
      Salt
      Freshly ground black pepper
    ¼ teaspoon cayenne pepper

Shred carrots with a grater or in a food processor using the julienne cutter. Blend together the remaining ingredients. Taste and correct seasonings. Pour over carrots and chill before serving. Yield: 8 to 10 servings.

Famous Recipe Salad Dressing Mix

    2 teaspoons salt
    2 to 3 teaspoons parsley flakes
    1 teaspoon garlic salt
    ½ teaspoon freshly ground black pepper
    ½ teaspoon onion powder
    1½ cups mayonnaise
    1¼ cups buttermilk

Mix together first five ingredients and store in a small, tightly covered container until needed. Combine 2 teaspoons of above mixture with remaining ingredients; taste and correct seasonings. For a thicker salad dressing, add more mayonnaise. Add more buttermilk for a thinner dressing. Yield: dressing for 3 salads.

Blender Mayonnaise

    2 egg yolks
    ¾ teaspoon salt
    ¼ teaspoon ground white or black pepper
    ½ teaspoon dry mustard
    ½ teaspoon paprika
    2 tablespoons lemon juice or wine vinegar
    1 cup vegetable oil

All ingredients must be at room temperature. Place all ingredients except juice and oil in blender. Cover and blend on low. When mixture is thick and foamy, add 1 tablespoon juice. Add half of the oil, drop by drop. Blend until thick; then run at high speed. Stop occasionally to scrape sides. Add remaining juice and with blender on high, slowly pour in remaining oil. Cover tightly and refrigerate; use within 1 week. Yield: 1 cup.

When lettuce is at its high winter price, the budget-conscious shopper should use more cabbage and canned vegetables in salads.

Salads and Vegetables

Welsh Onion-Potato Dish

  2 pounds potatoes, pared and sliced thin
1½ cups chopped onion
  4 tablespoons margarine
  1 teaspoon salt
    Freshly ground black pepper
    Pimiento, optional

Preheat oven to 350°. Layer about one-third of the potato slices into a well-greased 9 x 1½-inch pie plate and sprinkle with half the onion. Dot with butter and season lightly. Repeat, ending with a layer of potatoes, butter, and seasonings. Cover with foil and bake 1 hour. Remove foil, test for doneness. Bake up to 30 minutes longer or until lightly browned and tender. Yield: 6 servings.

Oriental Salad

10 ounces fresh spinach, washed and patted dry
  1 cup bean sprouts
  4 slices bacon, cooked and crumbled
  1 8-ounce can water chestnuts, drained and sliced

Toss above ingredients together lightly but thoroughly with Dressing in a large salad bowl. Serve immediately. Yield: 12 servings.

Dressing

½ cup vegetable oil
⅓ cup catsup
½ cup minced onion
½ teaspoon salt
¼ cup vinegar
 1 teaspoon Worcestershire sauce
   Freshly ground black pepper

Place dressing ingredients together in a jar with a lid. Close tightly and shake well. Pour on salad.

Quick Curried Vegetables

  2 tablespoons vegetable oil
  1 cup chopped onion
  2 large garlic cloves, minced
  1 green pepper, seeded and chopped
  1 cup sliced yellow summer squash
  2 cups sliced zucchini
  1 tablespoon water
  1 teaspoon curry powder
    Freshly ground black pepper
    Salt

Heat oil in a large frying pan. Add onion and garlic and sauté until onion begins to soften. Stir in remaining vegetables and water. Add seasonings to taste, cover and cook 5 to 10 minutes or until tender. Serve immediately with cooked brown rice. Yield: 4 servings.

Twice-Baked Potatoes

  5 baking potatoes
    Butter or margarine
  2 to 3 tablespoons hot milk or cream
  2 tablespoons raw wheat germ
½ cup grated sharp Cheddar cheese
    Paprika

Preheat oven to 400°. Butter skins of potatoes and puncture each a few times with a fork; bake 45 minutes to 1 hour or until tender. Slice each potato lengthwise; scoop out pulp into a medium-size bowl; mash. Stir in 3 to 4 tablespoons butter, hot milk, and wheat germ. Taste and season if needed. Beat until mixture is smooth; spoon back into potato cases. Top with the grated cheese, sprinkle with paprika. Cover with foil and bake for about 10 minutes or until piping hot and cheese is thoroughly melted. Yield: 10 servings.

Louise Lindsey's Cabbage Salad

  8 cups shredded cabbage
  2 carrots, shredded
  1 green pepper, minced
½ cup chopped onion
¾ cup cold water
  1 envelope unflavored gelatin
⅔ cup sugar
⅔ cup vinegar
  2 teaspoons celery seed
1½ teaspoons salt
¼ teaspoon freshly ground black pepper
⅔ cup vegetable oil

Mix cabbage, carrots, green pepper, and onion. Sprinkle with ½ cup cold water and chill. Soften gelatin in remaining water. Mix sugar, vinegar, celery seed, salt, and pepper in a saucepan. Bring to the boil. Stir in gelatin mixture; cool slightly until thickened. Beat in vegetable oil gradually. Drain cabbage mixture, place in serving bowl, and pour dressing over. Toss until cabbage mixture is well coated. Serve immediately or store in refrigerator until needed. Stir just before serving. Yield: 12 servings.

The handiest place to have an herb garden is right by the back door. Garlic, chives, sage, thyme, and mint will continue to grow year after year. Add parsley, fennel, dill, oregano, sweet basil, coriander, or whatever herbs you use most in cooking.

Desserts

Desserts need not be expensive, and sometimes they are the special treat that takes away the "sting" of a tight budget. Fresh fruit in season is always a smart dessert, but there are plenty of penny-wise desserts in this chapter to help meet your family's nutritional needs.

Irene's Superbars

½ cup margarine or butter
½ cup firmly packed brown sugar
½ cup rolled oats
½ cup whole wheat flour
½ cup unbleached flour
¼ cup raw wheat germ
1 teaspoon grated orange or lemon rind
1 teaspoon cinnamon
2 eggs
2 cups mixed dried fruits, nuts, and seeds and/or granola (such as raisins, cut dates, raw sunflower seeds, flaked coconut, walnuts, etc.)
2 tablespoons brown sugar

Preheat oven to 350°. Cream margarine and sugar together. Beat in oats, flours, rind, and wheat germ and cinnamon. Pat into 8 x 8 x 2-inch baking pan. Mix eggs, mixed fruits and nuts, and brown sugar together. Pour over base and spread evenly. Bake 30 to 35 minutes. Cool, then cut into 12 bars. Yield: 12 bars.

Aunt Ruby's Pinch Cookies

2 cups brown sugar, firmly packed
1 cup shortening
2 eggs
½ teaspoon salt
1 teaspoon baking soda
1 teaspoon vanilla
3 cups unbleached flour

Preheat oven to 350°. Cream sugar and shortening together thoroughly. Beat in eggs until light. Stir in the rest of the ingredients until well-blended. Pinch off pieces of dough the size of walnuts; roll and flatten with fingers and place on well-greased baking sheets. Bake 8 to 10 minutes or until done. Cool on wire racks. Yield: 4 dozen.

Mom's Prize-Winning Gingerbread

2 teaspoons vinegar stirred into ½ cup milk
½ cup margarine
½ cup brown sugar, firmly-packed
½ teaspoon ginger
1 egg
½ teaspoon cinnamon
¼ teaspoon salt
½ cup molasses
1¼ cups flour
1 teaspoon baking soda

Preheat oven to 350°. Allow vinegar and milk to clabber while mixing remaining ingredients, (except soda) in order. When ingredients are well-blended, dissolve soda in the clabbered milk and stir into flour mixture. Spread in greased 8 x 8 x 2-inch baking pan. Bake 20 to 25 minutes or until top springs back when touched lightly. Cool in pan on wire rack before cutting into squares. Yield: 16 squares.

Low-Cost Whipped Topping

¾ cup nonfat dried milk
¾ cup very cold water
½ teaspoon vanilla
Sugar

Chill beaters and bowl thoroughly; pour ingredients into bowl and whip until thick. Add vanilla and sugar, to taste. Yield: approximately 1 cup.

Cherry Pie

¾ cups granulated sugar
4 tablespoons whole wheat or unbleached flour
⅛ teaspoon salt
4 cups fresh, pitted cherries
or 2½ cups drained, canned cherries
¼ cup cherry juice
1 8-inch pastry crust plus extra pastry for strips or top crust

Preheat oven to 425°. Mix together sugar, flour, and salt. Stir in cherries and juice. Pour into pastry crust and cover with latticed strips or top crust. Seal edges. If top crust is used, slit to allow steam to escape. Bake for 10 minutes; then lower heat to 350° for 30 minutes or until done. Yield: 6 servings.

Banana Cream Cake

½ cup shortening
2 cups whole wheat pastry flour
1 cup firmly packed brown sugar
1½ teaspoons baking powder
1 teaspoon baking soda
1 teaspoon salt
½ teaspoon nutmeg
1 cup mashed, ripe banana
¼ cup milk
1 teaspoon vanilla
2 eggs
¼ cup chopped nuts, optional

Preheat oven to 350°. Cream shortening to soften. Stir in dry ingredients. Add banana, milk, and vanilla. Mix until dry ingredients are all moistened. Then beat vigorously for 2 minutes. Add eggs and beat 2 more minutes. Finally, add nuts and pour batter into a well-greased and lightly-floured 9 x 9 x 2-inch cake pan. Bake 35 to 40 minutes or until done. Yield: 9 to 12 servings.

Diana's Pie Crusts

3 cups flour
¾ teaspoon salt
1½ cups shortening
1 egg
1 tablespoon lemon juice
Water

Mix together flour and salt. Cut in shortening with a pastry blender until mixture resembles crumbs. Make a well in the center of the dry ingredients. In a measuring cup mix together the egg and lemon juice. Add enough water to make three-fourths cup liquid. Pour the egg mixture into the well in the dry ingredients. Mix with a fork until all the dry ingredients are moistened. Form the dough into a ball and chill until needed. Or divide the ball into thirds and roll out on a well-floured surface with a well-floured rolling pin. Both baked and unbaked crusts can be frozen, well-wrapped. Add fillings as desired and bake according to specific recipe directions. Yield: 3 9-inch crusts.

Vanilla Ice Cream

2 cups whole milk
½ cup non-instant powdered milk
¼ cup honey (or less, to taste)
1 teaspoon vanilla
1 rennet tablet
1 tablespoon cold water

Blend powdered milk with whole milk in a blender or with an electric beater or hand mixer. Pour into a heavy pan along with honey and vanilla and heat over medium heat until lukewarm (110°). While mixture is heating, dissolve rennet in cold water. When milk mixture is at lukewarm, add the rennet mixture and mix well. Pour quickly into ice cube tray or any other container that holds 2½ cups of liquid. Let stand at room temperature without disturbing for 10 minutes. Place tray in freezer compartment and freeze until almost totally firm. Break up mixture in a large mixing bowl and quickly beat until smooth. Pour immediately back into tray and finish freezing. Serve plain or with crushed fruit, nuts, sesame seeds, sunflower seeds, or with Peanut Butter Sauce. Yield: 1 pint.

Peanut Butter Sauce

¾ cup non-hydrogenated peanut butter
1 tablespoon honey
¼ cup whole, salted peanuts
2 tablespoons sunflower seeds
2 tablespoons sesame seeds
½ teaspoon vanilla

Gently mix together ingredients. Spoon into small, heavy pan and place over extremely low heat. Stir continuously. When warmed and well-blended, serve on ice cream. Yield: about 1 cup.

Rhubarb Cream Pie

1¼ cups brown sugar, firmly packed
3 tablespoons whole wheat or unbleached flour
½ teaspoon nutmeg
1 tablespoon butter
2 well-beaten eggs
3 cups cut up rhubarb
1 9-inch pastry crust

Preheat oven to 425°. Blend first 4 ingredients together thoroughly. Add eggs. Finally, stir in rhubarb. Sprinkle more nutmeg on top, if desired. Bake for 10 minutes; then lower heat to 350° and bake for 30 more minutes or until done. Yield: 6 to 8 servings.

Desserts

Whole Wheat Fruitcake

2¼ cups whole wheat flour
¼ cup soy flour
¼ cup raw wheat germ
1 teaspoon baking soda
2 eggs, lightly beaten
3½ cups mincemeat
1 14-ounce can sweetened condensed milk
¾ cup walnuts, hickory nuts, or mixed nuts
¼ cup sunflower seeds
2 cups candied peel

Preheat oven to 300°. Mix together flours, wheat germ, and soda. Combine eggs, mincemeat, milk, nuts, and fruit. Fold dry ingredients into wet. Pour into well-greased 9-inch tube pan or spring-form. Bake for 2 hours or until center springs back when touched lightly and top is golden. Cool before turning out. Yield: 1 large fruitcake.

Note: This recipe can be baked in several smaller cake pans or baking molds. Reduce baking time, checking frequently for doneness.

Candied Fruit Peel

2 cups mixed grapefruit, orange, lime, and lemon peel
1½ cups cold water
1 cup sugar
½ cup water

Cut peel into very thin strips and place in a heavy pan. Cover with cold water and bring slowly to a boil. Reduce heat and simmer 10 to 12 minutes, drain and repeat process about 4 times or until peel has lost its bitter taste. Combine sugar and ½ cup water, making a syrup, and add peel. Boil gently until all syrup is absorbed and peel is transparent. Watch carefully to keep from burning. Spread on racks to dry. Yield: about 2 cups.

On cold winter days when the wind is howling, why not turn down the heat in the rest of the house, close the doors to the kitchen, and bake? Keeping the oven filled with various dishes that need to be cooked at the same temperature will use energy well—and keep the cook warm!

Because moisture content in flour varies, always test-bake one cookie to make certain there is enough flour in the dough before baking the whole batch.

Aunt Ruth's Icebox Cookies

1¾ cups brown sugar, firmly packed
1 cup shortening or margarine
2 eggs
1 teaspoon baking soda, dissolved in 2 tablespoons water
1 teaspoon cinnamon
2 teaspoons vanilla
4 cups unbleached flour
½ teaspoon salt
¾ cup chopped nuts or raisins
1 cup Flaked Coconut, optional (page 60)

Cream sugar and shortening together thoroughly. Beat in eggs until light. Add soda-water mixture, cinnamon, and vanilla. Stir flour and salt together and mix in thoroughly. Finally, add nuts or raisins. Roll dough into 2 12-inch long rolls; wrap and chill until ready to bake. Preheat oven to 350°; slice rolls into ¼-inch slices and place on greased baking sheets. Bake 8 to 10 minutes or until done. Cool on wire racks. Yield: approximately 8 dozen.

Mom's Apple-Bran Cake

1 cup brown sugar, firmly packed
½ cup (1 stick) margarine
2 eggs
1½ cups unbleached flour
2 teaspoons baking soda
½ teaspoon salt
1 teaspoon cinnamon
1 teaspoon grated nutmeg
1 cup bran flakes
4 cups chopped apples
Cream Cheese Icing

Preheat oven to 350°. Cream sugar and margarine together thoroughly. Add eggs and beat until light and fluffy. Mix together dry ingredients and stir into egg mixture, beating well. Finally, fold in chopped apples well. Pour into a well-greased 9 x 9-inch cake pan and bake for 45 minutes or until top springs back when touched lightly. Cool on wire rack. Spread with Cream Cheese Icing.

Cream Cheese Icing

1 3-ounce package cream cheese, softened
1 tablespoon margarine
1 teaspoon vanilla
1½ cups confectioners' sugar

Blend ingredients together thoroughly and spread onto cake.

Desserts

Applesauce Cake

    1 cup firmly packed brown sugar
    ½ cup (1 stick) margarine
    2 eggs (at room temperature)
    2 cups whole wheat pastry flour or unbleached flour
    2 teaspoons baking soda
    ¼ teaspoon salt
    ¼ cup raw wheat germ
    2 cups thick applesauce
    ½ cup apple cider
    ½ cup chopped nuts, optional
      Confectioners' sugar

All ingredients should be at room temperature. Preheat oven to 325°. Cream sugar and margarine together until light; beat in eggs thoroughly. Stir in remaining ingredients except ¼ cup cider and nuts and beat at medium speed for 3 minutes, scraping the sides of the bowl regularly. Stir in nuts. Pour batter into 9 x 5 x 3-inch loaf pan. Bake for 1½ hours or until center springs back when lightly touched. Cool in pan for 10 minutes on a wire rack; remove. If desired, spoon remaining cider onto cake. Cool cake completely and sprinkle with confectioners' sugar. Yield: 1 loaf cake.

Mincemeat Cookies

    ¾ cup shortening
    1 cup granulated sugar
    3 eggs
    3 cups unbleached flour
    ¾ teaspoon salt
    1 teaspoon baking soda
    1 teaspoon cinnamon
    1 teaspoon allspice
    1 cup mincemeat
      Rind of 1 lemon, grated
    ¾ cup chopped nuts
    ½ cup raisins

Preheat oven to 350°. Cream together shortening and sugar. Beat in eggs until light and fluffy. Mix dry ingredients. Add half the dry ingredients to the egg mixture. Stir in mincemeat and lemon rind. Add remaining dry ingredients and mix thoroughly. Stir in nuts and raisins. Drop by teaspoonfuls on greased baking sheets. Bake for 10 minutes or until done. Yield: 4 dozen cookies.

Look for more excellent dessert recipes in the "Timesaving Basic Mixes" chapter.

Fudge Sheet Cake

    2 cups unbleached flour or whole wheat pastry flour
    1½ cups granulated sugar
    1 cup (2 sticks) margarine
    7 tablespoons cocoa
    1 cup water
    ½ cup milk soured with 1½ teaspoons vinegar
    1 teaspoon baking soda
    2 eggs, lightly beaten
    1 teaspoon vanilla

Preheat oven to 375°. Combine flour and sugar in a large mixing bowl. Place margarine, cocoa, and water into a small, heavy saucepan and heat to boiling, stirring regularly. Blend with flour mixture thoroughly. Mix soda with soured milk and combine with eggs and vanilla. Stir the milk mixture into the flour mixture until thoroughly blended. Pour mixture into a jelly-roll pan (10 x 15 x 1-inch) that has been lightly greased and floured. Bake about 20 minutes. Prepare icing during last few minutes of baking time. Cake is done when pick inserted in center comes out clean. Remove cake from oven, and immediately pour hot icing on top, spreading evenly. Cool before serving. Yield: 2 dozen servings.

Icing

    ½ cup (1 stick) margarine
    4 tablespoons cocoa
    6 tablespoons milk
    1 pound confectioners' sugar, sifted
    1 cup chopped nuts, optional

Place margarine, cocoa, and milk in a medium-size, heavy saucepan and heat to boiling, stirring, regularly. Stir in sugar, nuts and mix well.

Charlotte's Quick Fruit Dessert

    ¼ cup margarine
    ¾ cup milk
    ½ cup brown sugar, firmly packed
    1 cup whole wheat pastry flour or unbleached flour
    1½ teaspoons baking powder
    2 cups freshly sliced apples, berries, etc.
    1 teaspoon cinnamon or nutmeg, optional

Preheat oven to 350°. Melt margarine in bottom of 8 x 8-inch pan placed in oven. Combine milk, sugar, flour, and baking powder. Stir slightly, just moistening ingredients. Pour mixture evenly onto melted margarine. Don't stir. Pour fruit evenly over batter; push apple slices into batter slightly. Sprinkle on cinnamon or nutmeg, if desired. Bake about 1 hour or until done. Serve hot or cold. Yield: 12 servings.

Zucchini Bars

- ¾ cup soft margarine or butter
- ½ cup brown sugar, firmly packed
- 2 eggs
- 1 teaspoon vanilla
- 1¾ cups whole wheat flour
- ½ teaspoon salt
- 1½ teaspoons baking powder
- ¾ cup dates, finely chopped
- ¾ cup raisins, optional
- 2 cups raw, unpeeled, grated zucchini
  Chopped nuts, optional

Preheat oven to 350°. Cream together margarine and sugar. Add egg and vanilla and beat until light. Stir together flour, salt, and baking powder and add to creamed ingredients. Finally, add dried fruit and zucchini. Spoon into a greased 10 x 13-inch cake pan and bake for 35 to 40 minutes or until top springs back. While still warm, spread glaze evenly over bars. Sprinkle with chopped nuts if desired. Bars can be frozen. Yield: 15 to 18 bars.

Glaze

- 1 tablespoon margarine, softened
- 1 cup confectioners' sugar
- ¼ teaspoon cinnamon
- 1 teaspoon vanilla
- 1 to 2 tablespoons milk
- ½ cup chopped nuts, optional

Mix to desired consistency.

Mom's Miracle Brownies

- ¾ cup unbleached flour
- ¾ cup granulated sugar
- ½ teaspoon baking powder
- 7 tablespoons cocoa
- ¾ teaspoon salt
- ⅔ cup shortening
- 2 eggs
- 1 teaspoon vanilla
- 1 tablespoon honey
- 1 cup chopped nuts

Preheat oven to 350°. Sift flour, sugar, baking powder, cocoa, and salt together into a medium-size mixing bowl. Beat in remaining ingredients, in order, mixing well after each addition. Finally, stir in nuts. Spread into a greased 8 x 8 x 2-inch baking pan and bake for 30 to 40 minutes, or until done. Cool in pan before slicing into squares. Yield: 16 squares.

Apple-Candied Peel Bars

- 2 cups unbleached flour
- 1 teaspoon baking powder
- ¼ teaspoon ground cloves
- 2 teaspoons cinnamon
- 2 eggs
- ¾ cup firmly packed brown sugar
- 2 tablespoons water
- 1 teaspoon rum flavoring
- ¼ cup Candied Peel, (page 38)
- ⅔ cup chopped almonds
- 1 apple, chopped

Preheat oven to 350°. Mix first 4 ingredients together. In a separate bowl, beat eggs well; stir in brown sugar, water, and rum flavoring. When thoroughly blended, mix dry ingredients with egg mixture. Finally, stir in peel, almonds, and apple. Spread in a well-greased 9 x 13-inch baking pan or in miniature muffin tins to make small "fruit cakes." Bake for 20 minutes or until done. Glaze, if desired. Yield: 20 bars.

Glaze:

- 1 cup confectioners' sugar
- ¾ teaspoon rum flavoring
- 1½ tablespoons water

Blend glaze ingredients together until smooth. Glaze bars while still warm. Cool thoroughly before cutting into squares.

Kate's Self-Frosting Cake

- ½ cup margarine
- 1 cup brown sugar, firmly packed
- 1 cup unbleached flour
- ½ cup whole wheat flour
- 1 teaspoon baking powder
- 1 egg
- 1 8½-ounce can crushed pineapple
- ½ cup granulated sugar
- ½ cup Flaked Coconut (page 60)
  Chopped nuts, optional

Preheat oven to 350°. Cream margarine and brown sugar together thoroughly. Add flours, baking powder, egg, and pineapple. Stir well. Spread into a greased 8 x 8 x 2-inch baking pan. Mix sugar, coconut, and nuts, and sprinkle evenly on top of cake. Bake for 30 to 35 minutes or until done. Yield: 16 squares.

Karl's Pumpkin Cookies

- 1 cup margarine, softened
- ¾ cup brown sugar, firmly-packed
- 2¼ cups whole wheat pastry flour or unbleached flour
- ¼ cup raw wheat germ
- 1 tablespoon baking powder
- 1½ teaspoons salt (if pumpkin is salted, use less)
- 2 teaspoons allspice
- 1 teaspoon cinnamon
- 2 eggs
- 1 cup canned or cooked pumpkin
- 2 cups old-fashioned rolled oats
- 1 teaspoon vanilla
- ½ cup (or more) raisins or currants
- ¼ cup (or more) chopped nuts

Preheat oven to 350°. Cream together margarine and brown sugar. Combine dry ingredients. Add eggs to margarine mixture and beat until light. Add pumpkin. Stir in dry ingredients; add rolled oats and vanilla and stir thoroughly. Finally, add fruit and nuts. Drop by teaspoonfuls onto greased cookie sheets and bake 8 to 10 minutes or until lightly browned and top springs back when touched lightly. Cool on wire racks. Yield: approximately 6 dozen.

Rolled-Out Ginger Cookies

- 1 cup margarine, softened
- ¾ cup brown sugar, firmly-packed
- 1 egg
- 1 cup old-fashioned molasses
- 2 tablespoons vinegar
- 1½ teaspoons baking soda
- ½ teaspoon salt
- 1 tablespoon ginger
- 1 teaspoon cinnamon
- 1 teaspoon allspice
- 3 cups whole wheat flour
- 1¾ cups unbleached flour
- ¼ cup soy flour
- Raisins or currants, optional

Cream together margarine and sugar. Beat in egg, molasses, vinegar, soda, salt and spices. Stir in flours. Chill thoroughly. Preheat oven to 375°. On a well-floured surface, roll with a well-floured rolling pin to ⅛ inch . Cut into shapes. If desired, decorate with raisins and currants. Place on greased baking sheet. Bake for 6 minutes or until done. Remove from pan to wire rack for cooling. Decorate with icing and other decorations, if desired. Yield: 8 dozen small to medium cookies.

Cheesecake
Crust

- ⅔ cup vanilla wafer cookie crumbs
- 1 tablespoon soy flour
- 1 tablespoon sunflower seeds
- ½ teaspoon cinnamon
- 2 teaspoons honey
- 2 tablespoons margarine, melted

Mix together crumbs, soy flour, cinnamon, and sunflower seeds. Stir in honey and margarine until all crumbs are moistened. Press crumbs against the sides and bottom of a 9-inch pie plate which holds 4 cups. Reserve any extra crumbs. Chill until ready to use. Yield: 6 to 8 servings.

Filling

- 1 envelope unflavored gelatin
- 1 tablespoon lemon juice
- Peel of ½ lemon
- ½ cup hot milk
- ¼ cup honey
- 2 egg yolks
- 1 8-ounce package cream cheese, softened
- 1 cup creamed cottage cheese, drained, or sour cream
- 1 cup crushed ice

Place gelatin, lemon juice, peel, milk, and honey in an electric blender. Cover and blend. Add egg yolks and cream cheese and blend, covered, for 10 seconds. Add cottage cheese and ice. Cover and blend until smooth. Pour mixture into crumb crust. Any leftover crumbs could be sprinkled on top, or garnished with toasted wheat germ.

Grandma Earle's Apple Bars

- 3 tablespoons margarine, softened
- ¾ cup brown sugar, firmly-packed
- 1 teaspoon vanilla
- 1 egg
- ½ teaspoon salt
- 1 teaspoon baking powder
- 1 teaspoon cinnamon
- 1 cup unbleached or whole wheat pastry flour
- 3 cups chopped apples
- ½ cup chopped nuts

Preheat oven to 350°. Beat margarine, sugar, vanilla, and egg together thoroughly. Mix dry ingredients and stir in until completely blended. Finally, stir in apples and nuts. Pour into a lightly greased 7½ x 9-inch baking pan and bake for 30 minutes or until top springs back when touched lightly. Cool on wire rack. Yield: 12 servings.

Economical Entertaining

Entertain well without anyone else knowing that the budget is being carefully watched. At dinner parties try some economical dishes from foreign lands—Italian pasta or a Chinese chicken dish or an Indonesian Rijsttafel (rice table) plus an interesting salad will make everyone think the hostess (or host) is a gourmet cook, and without a huge cash outlay. A fresh loaf of homemade bread will probably bring more raves than anything else. Soup is often a moneysaver, yet as a first course it seems very elegant. Check the index for interesting foods from the same country or from a number of countries.

Joyce's Stuffed Shells

    2 12-ounce packages jumbo shell macaroni
       or cannelloni or manicotti shells
    2 quarts (64-ounces) Grandma Benvenuto's
       Tomato Sauce (page 47)
    4 10-ounce packages frozen chopped spinach or
       3 pounds lightly steamed fresh spinach or chard
    4 eggs, lightly beaten
    2 pounds small curd cottage cheese or ricotta
    1 pound shredded mozzarella cheese
    ¼ teaspoon nutmeg
    ⅓ cup freshly grated Parmesan cheese

Cook shells according to package directions until just tender. (Overcooking them will cause them to break apart during stuffing.) Heat spaghetti sauce to simmer. Thaw spinach and drain thoroughly. Mix eggs, cottage cheese, mozzarella, and nutmeg together until well-blended. Stir in spinach and stuff shells with 2 teaspoonsful of the spinach mixture. Preheat oven to 350°. Pour one-fourth of the spaghetti sauce into the bottom of a flat casserole dish that will hold three quarts. Arrange stuffed shells in a single layer on top of the sauce. Pour part of the remaining sauce over shells, leaving enough to repeat process with a second casserole dish. When both casserole dishes are prepared, sprinkle both with Parmesan cheese and bake for 30 minutes or until heated through. One or both of the casserole dishes can be frozen after assembling. Cover ovenproof dish or pan tightly with foil. An hour before needed, preheat oven to 425° and bake frozen casseroles for 40 minutes. Remove foil and bake 20 minutes more or until done. Yield: 12 servings.

Diana's Desperation Burritos

    2 cups leftover chicken, browned ground beef,
       tuna, etc.
    ½ cup chopped onion (green onion, if in season)
    1 16-ounce can refried beans
    ½ 10½-ounce can mushroom soup
    ½ cup taco sauce (more or less, to taste)
    8 to 12 tortillas
    ¾ pound shredded Colby cheese

Preheat oven to 350°. Mix together first 5 ingredients and heat until warm. Separate tortillas (heat, if necessary to keep from cracking when rolling up). Divide meat mixture among tortillas, spreading the mixture along just one edge. Divide the cheese among tortillas, sprinkling on top of meat mixture. Roll up and place on greased baking sheet. Bake for 20 to 25 minutes or until cheese melts and burritos are heated through. Yield: 8 to 12 servings.

Baked Fish Soufflé

    1½ pounds fresh or frozen fish fillets, thawed
    1 teaspoon salt
    ¼ teaspoon freshly ground black pepper
    1 teaspoon butter or margarine
    2 egg whites
    ¼ cup mayonnaise
    3 tablespoons onion, minced (preferably green
       onions, if in season)
    1 tablespoon pickle relish
    1 tablespoon minced parsley
    ¼ teaspoon salt
    2 to 3 drops bottled red pepper sauce

Preheat oven to 425°. Place fillets in a greased baking dish; sprinkle with salt and pepper and pat with butter. Bake for 10 minutes. Beat egg whites until stiff but not dry. Blend in remaining ingredients and spread over hot fish, covering completely. Continue baking 10 to 15 minutes longer until topping is puffy and fish flakes easily with a fork. Yield: 4 servings.

Sherbos' Seven Layer Dinner

- 2 tablespoons oil
- ½ pound ground beef or turkey
- 1 cup chopped onion
- 2 cups thinly sliced raw potatoes
- ½ cup raw brown rice
- 1 green pepper, chopped
- 2 cups shredded carrots
- ½ cup sliced onion
- 1½ cups diced celery
- ½ cup raw wheat germ
- 4 cups tomato juice or canned tomatoes in juice
  Freshly ground black pepper
  Salt

Preheat oven to 350° or use slow cooker. Brown ground beef and chopped onion lightly in hot oil. Place potatoes in bottom of 3-quart casserole dish or slow cooker. Sprinkle rice on top of potatoes evenly. Follow, in layers, with meat mixture, green pepper, carrots, sliced onion, and celery and top with wheat germ. Taste tomato juice and add salt and pepper to season well. Pour juice over all. Cover tightly and bake 2 hours or until done in oven—8 hours on low in slow cooker. Yield: 8 servings.

Sweet 'N' Sour Pork

- 2 pounds lean pork (shoulder, loin blade chops, or most reasonable cut available)
- ¼ cup water
- 2½ cups (20-ounce can) pineapple chunks
- 2 tablespoons cornstarch
- ¼ cup brown sugar, firmly-packed
- ¼ cup cider vinegar
- 2 tablespoons soy sauce
- ⅓ cup thinly sliced onion rings
- 1 cup green and red pepper rings
- ½ cup bamboo shoots, drained, optional
  Salt

Slice any fat off pork and cut meat into bite-size chunks. Render fat in large skillet. Remove and add meat. Stir-fry pork until browned. Add water; cover and simmer 60 minutes or until tender. Meanwhile, drain pineapple, saving juice. Combine cornstarch and sugar; stir in vinegar until well-blended. Add pineapple juice and soy sauce. Stir into pork and cook, stirring constantly, until sauce is thickened. Add onion and pepper rings; stir lightly. Finally add pineapple chunks and bamboo shoots. Cook 2 to 3 minutes or until heated through. Correct seasonings. Serve over hot rice or chow mein noodles. Yield: 6 to 8 servings.

Chicken Satay

- 2 pounds chicken breasts, cut into bite-size strips
- 3 tablespoons chopped onion
- 1 tablespoon peanut or vegetable oil
- 2 cloves garlic, minced
- ¼ teaspoon ground cardamom
- ⅔ cup plus 1 tablespoon crunchy peanut butter
- 1 teaspoon turmeric
- 2 teaspoons ground coriander
- 1½ teaspoons ground cumin
- 1 teaspoon red pepper flakes, soaked in a small amount of warm water
- 1 tablespoon lemon juice
- 1 teaspoon salt
- 1 tablespoon brown sugar
- ½ cup water

Thread chicken pieces on wooden skewers. Make marinade by stirring together 1 tablespoon peanut butter and remaining ingredients. Place chicken pieces in marinade and leave overnight. Remove skewered chicken and barbecue 3 to 4 minutes outdoors (basting constantly) or broil indoors until browned. Keep chicken hot. To prepare sauce add remaining peanut buttter and enough water to remaining leftover marinade to make a sauce of desired consistency. Simmer for 5 minutes and serve hot with the skewered chicken. Yield: 8 servings.

Szechuan Beef (Hot Chinese Dish)

- 2 pounds lean, low-cost beef
- 4 tablespoons soy sauce
- 3 tablespoons dry sherry
- ⅛ teaspoon cayenne pepper
- 2 carrots, sliced on the diagonal
- 1 stalk celery, sliced on the diagonal
- 2 light green chili peppers, seeded and sliced
- 1 sweet green pepper, cut in strips
- 5 large cloves garlic, minced

Trim fat off beef; slice beef into thin, bite-size pieces. Render beef fat in a skillet; stir in beef and cook until brown. Stir in soy sauce and sherry. Cover and simmer until beef is very tender (1 hour or more). Stir in vegetables and cook briefly (they should be crisp). Taste and correct seasonings. Serve over rice. Yield: 6 to 8 servings.

A FAVORITE RECIPE FOR "Blair's chicken"
With orange sauce
1 Broiler-fryer, cut up
1/2 c. white instant flour
1/2 c. orange juice
4 t. dry mustard
1/2 t. salt, paprika
dash bottled hot pepper sauce
orange marmalade
oil mushrooms (sliced)

Blair's Chicken with Orange Sauce

1 fryer, cut up
½ cup whole wheat flour
½ cup orange juice
¼ teaspoon dry mustard
½ teaspoon paprika
½ teaspoon salt
⅛ teaspoon bottled hot pepper sauce
⅓ cup orange marmalade
¼ cup vegetable oil
1 pound Braised Mushrooms

Preheat oven to 325°. Coat chicken with flour. Mix remaining ingredients, except mushrooms, together thoroughly. Place chicken in a shallow baking dish and pour sauce over. Bake for 2 hours, basting regularly. The last 15 minutes add mushrooms and stir in thoroughly. Yield: 4 servings.

Braised Mushrooms

2 tablespoons margarine
1 pound mushrooms, washed and patted dry
Salt
Freshly ground black pepper

Melt margarine in a large frying pan. Stir in mushrooms and allow to simmer, covered, in their own juice until just tender. Add salt and pepper to taste. Eat as is or use in Blair's Chicken with Orange Sauce recipe.

Indonesian Beef

Suet or 1 tablespoon vegetable oil
3 pounds lean beef, cut into bite-size pieces
1 cup chopped onion
4 cloves garlic, minced
1 tablespoon fresh, grated ginger
½ teaspoon cinnamon
½ teaspoon nutmeg
½ teaspoon cardamom
¼ teaspoon ground cloves
1 teaspoon brown sugar
1 cup beef broth
2 tablespoons soy sauce
Salt
Freshly ground black pepper

Render suet in a large frying pan; add beef cubes and sauté until brown. Add onion and garlic toward end of browning period. Add ginger and other spices, brown sugar, beef broth, and soy sauce. Bring to simmer, cover and simmer 1½ hours until beef is tender. Taste and correct seasoning. Serve with rice and Hot Pepper and Celery Sambal. Yield: 8 servings.

Ham Stuffed Crepes

3 tablespoons margarine
5 tablespoons unbleached flour
2 cups milk
Salt
Freshly ground black pepper
2 cups ground ham
10 Crepes (page 27)

Melt margarine in a heavy-bottomed saucepan. Stir in flour and allow to cook, stirring regularly, for a few minutes until flour is golden. Pour in milk all at once. Stir with a wire whisk until sauce thickens. Add salt and a good deal of pepper, to taste. Mix one cup of the cream sauce with ham. Divide ham mixture among the crepes and place crepes in a well-buttered casserole dish. Pour remaining sauce over the crepes, cover with aluminum foil, and refrigerate until approximately 40 minutes before serving. Preheat oven to 350°. Bake crepes approximately 40 minutes or until very hot. Leave foil off the last 5 to 10 minutes to brown surface as desired. Yield: 10 crepes.

Grandma Benvenuto's Tomato Sauce

¼ cup olive oil
½ pound bulk pork sausage
1 pound ground beef
3 minced garlic cloves
½ green pepper, minced
1 onion, minced
2 12-ounce cans tomato paste
3 28-ounce cans tomatoes
3 bay leaves
3 tablespoons salt
1 tablespoon oregano
1 tablespoon sugar

In a very large, heavy-bottomed saucepan or Dutch oven heat olive oil. Stir in sausage, reduce heat and cook for 30 minutes. Add ground beef, garlic, pepper, and onion. Turn up heat and brown meat quickly. Place tomato paste and tomatoes in blender and blend until smooth. Pour tomato sauce over meat mixture and bring to boil. Reduce heat and simmer. Add remaining ingredients. Simmer from 1 to 3 hours. Sauce can be used on pasta, on pizza, or in casseroles. It can be stored in refrigerator for up to a week or can be frozen for use later. Yield: approximately 4 quarts.

Economical Entertaining

Indonesian Curried Pork

    Pork fat *or* 2 tablespoons vegetable oil
2½ to 3 pounds lean pork, cut into bite-size pieces
    ¼ cup flour
    3 cups chopped onion
    5 cloves garlic, minced
    2 to 3 tablespoons curry powder
    2 cups Coconut Milk (page 60)
    2 strips lemon or lime peel
    2 strips orange peel
      Salt
      Freshly ground black pepper

Render pork fat in a large frying pan (or heat oil). Meanwhile, roll pork cubes in flour until well-covered. Brown pork well; add onion and garlic toward end of browning period. Stir in coconut milk and seasonings. Reduce heat, cover, and simmer 1½ hours or more until pork is tender. Skim fat. Taste and correct seasonings. Serve at this point or cool and freeze, well wrapped. Reheat thoroughly before serving with Minted, Parslied Rice and Hot Pepper and Celery Sambal, if desired. Yield: 6 to 8 servings.

Minted, Parslied Rice

    5 cups water
    1 tablespoon margarine
    2 cups long-grained rice
    ¼ cup chopped mint
    ¼ cup chopped parsley
      Salt
      Freshly ground black pepper

Bring water and margarine to boiling point in a heavy-bottomed saucepan. Stir in rice, cover, reduce heat, and simmer 15 to 18 minutes or until water is absorbed and rice is tender. Turn off heat and let stand for about 5 minutes before fluffing with a fork and gently stirring in mint, parsley, and seasonings. If desired, pack rice into a buttered mold and unmold just before serving on a platter garnished with parsley. Yield: 6 to 8 servings.

Hot Chocolate Mix

    ½ cup cocoa
    ¾ cup sugar
      Dash salt
    3 cups nonfat dry milk

Mix ingredients together thoroughly and store in tightly covered container. When hot chocolate is desired, use ¼ to ⅓ cup mix to 1 cup water. Heat, stirring with a wire whisk, until foamy and thoroughly blended. Yield: 2 quarts.

Sangria

    1 orange, sliced
    1 lime, sliced
    1 lemon, sliced
    ¼ cup granulated sugar
    ½ cup brandy
    1 bottle (24-ounce) Spanish red wine or
      California Burgundy
    2 tablespoons lemon juice
    3 cups soda water

Place sliced fruit into a very large pitcher. Mix sugar and brandy together until sugar dissolves and pour over fruit. Let stand at room temperature for an hour. Pour in red wine and lemon juice, stir, and let stand another hour. Just before serving, add ice cubes and soda water. Stir until thoroughly chilled and serve. Yield: 8 servings.

Claret Punch

    4 cups ginger ale
    2 bottles claret wine
    2 6-ounce cans lemonade concentrate
    2 cups pineapple juice
    1 orange, sliced

Pour ginger ale into a 1-gallon container. Add remaining ingredients, stirring well. Finally, add enough ice cubes to fill the container. Stir until well chilled and serve. Yield: 1 gallon.

Hot Apple Tea

    1 quart (4 cups) apple juice
    4 teaspoons loose tea leaves
    1 lemon, sliced
    1 apple, sliced
    6 cinnamon sticks or ½ teaspoon cinnamon

Heat apple juice until just boiling; pour over tea leaves in a scalded teapot. Steep 2 to 3 minutes. Serve with lemon and apple slices and garnish with cinnamon. Yield: 6 servings.

Why not serve "tea" at four o' clock some afternoon? Along with freshly brewed tea in china cups, serve tiny sandwiches, a thinly sliced cake, a quick bread (with butter and jam on the side), and a few tempting cookies.

Wine tasting parties are fun. Ask each guest to bring a bottle of good wine for everyone to sample in polished wine glasses. The hosts provide a good selection of cheeses and crackers or breads.

Canning and Freezing

There is no question that a way to save an enormous amount on food is to plant a vegetable garden. For a very small cash outlay, it's possible to grow delicious fresh carrots, Swiss chard, green beans, and tomatoes—all prolific—even in a minuscule plot. Plant family favorites, learn to can and freeze them, and reap huge savings. Eat frozen green peppers during the winter when they are selling at out-of-season prices and experience one of the many joys of gardening.

Hints:

1. Freeze as soon after harvesting as possible.
2. Freeze only ripe, unblemished fruits and tender vegetables.
3. Most vegetables must be scalded, using 1 gallon of water for every pint of vegetables. Bring water to boil in a large kettle with cover; place washed and prepared vegetable into boiling water in a colander or wire basket and submerge until vegetable is heated to the center. (See chart.) Remove from boiling water immediately and plunge vegetable into ice water. Drain and pack into freezer containers. Leave head space for vegetables that pack down.

Sliced Cucumber Pickles

8 cups very thinly sliced cucumbers
¼ cup pickling salt
   Ice cubes
4 cups very thinly sliced small onions
2 cups cider vinegar
1½ cups sugar
2 teaspoons celery seed
1 tablespoon mustard seed
2 teaspoons ginger
1 teaspoon turmeric

Place cucumber slices in a large bowl; sprinkle with salt and toss gently. Cover with ice cubes and let stand 2 to 3 hours or until cucumbers are thoroughly crisped. Drain and stir in onions. Combine remaining ingredients in a large, heavy-bottomed saucepan. Bring to a boil and allow to boil for 10 minutes. Stir in cucumber and onion slices and allow to return to boiling. Pack at once in hot, sterilized jars, and seal. Process in boiling water bath for 30 minutes. Remove and cool before storing. Yield: 4 pints.

Guide to Freezing Garden Produce

Berries: blackberries, boysenberries, loganberries, blueberries.	Wash in ice water; drain carefully; pack and freeze.
Cherries (tart)	Wash, stem, and pit. Stir ¾ cup sugar into each quart of cherries until sugar dissolves. Package and freeze.
Green or yellow beans	Scald 3½ minutes. Package and freeze.
Greens: collards, Swiss chard, beet or turnip greens, kale, spinach	Use 2 gallons water per pint of greens. Scald all greens except collards and chard stems for 2 minutes. Scald collards and chard stems 3 to 4 minutes. Package and freeze.
Peas	Scald shelled peas 1½ to 2 minutes. Package and freeze.
Peppers	Can be frozen without scalding for use in casseroles and other cooked dishes.
Pumpkin and winter squash	Cut into uniform pieces and either steam or bake at 350° until tender. Scoop pulp from shells, puree, and package. Freeze.
Rhubarb	Cut off leaves and ends. Wash and cut into 1-inch pieces or freeze whole.
Strawberries	Wash in cold water, drain, hull, and slice into thirds. Use 1 cup sugar for every 9 cups berries. Stir carefully to dissolve sugar, pack and freeze.
Summer squash: zucchini, crookneck	Wash, do not peel, cut into 1¼-inch pieces and scald 6 minutes.
Tomatoes	Whole tomatoes or uncooked tomato pulp (to be used in casseroles and other cooked dishes) can be frozen without scalding if used within a few months of freezing.

Canning and Freezing

Emma Rogers' Frozen Coleslaw

1 very large head cabbage, shredded
1 teaspoon salt
1 cup vinegar
2 cups sugar (or much less if vinegar isn't tart)
¼ cup water
1 teaspoon celery seed
1 teaspoon mustard seed
1 mango, and/or pimiento, cut-up, optional
  Shredded carrots, diced celery, optional

Toss cabbage with salt and drain. Mix together vinegar, sugar, water, celery and mustard seed in a heavy-bottomed saucepan. Bring to the boil and boil for 1 minute. Cool. Pour over drained, shredded cabbage in a large mixing bowl. Package in freezer containers as desired and freeze. Remove approximately ½ hour before serving to thaw and serve garnished with optional ingredients listed above. Yield: 10 servings.

Chowchow

1 medium head cabbage, chopped
4 cups chopped cucumbers
6 green peppers, seeded and chopped
4 cups chopped green tomatoes
¼ cup pickling salt
2 teaspoons dry mustard
6 cups cider vinegar
2½ cups sugar
1 teaspoon turmeric
1 teaspoon ginger
1 tablespoon mustard seed
1 tablespoon celery seed
1 tablespoon mixed whole pickling spices

Combine vegetables and mix with salt. Cover and let stand overnight. Drain juices. Mix mustard with 1 tablespoon of vinegar into a smooth paste. Add to remaining vinegar in a large, heavy kettle along with remaining ingredients, except cabbage mixture. Simmer for 20 minutes; add cabbage mixture. Simmer 10 minutes more. Simmer remainder while packing relish into hot, sterilized jars. Fill within ⅛-inch of the top, being certain liquid covers pickles. Wipe jar lid clean and seal with sterilized ring and lid. Repeat until all relish is used. Yield: 6 to 9 pints.

Note: Vegetables can be put through medium-fine blade of grinder, if preferred.

Julia's Bread and Butter Pickles

4 quarts medium-size pickling cucumbers, chilled
3 to 4 cups small white onions, sliced very thin
2 green or red peppers, chopped
½ cup pickling salt
5 cups cider vinegar
5 cups brown sugar
1½ teaspoons allspice
2 tablespoons mustard seed
1½ teaspoons celery seeds
½ teaspoon ground cloves or one 1-inch stick cinnamon

Slice chilled cucumbers into the thinnest slices possible. Place vegetables in a bowl and sprinkle salt over all. Cover with a weighted lid and place in refrigerator for three hours. Rinse in ice water. Drain well. Mix vinegar, sugar, and spices together in a large, heavy kettle and bring to the boiling point. Add vegetables gradually with very little stirring. Heat to scalding point but do not permit to boil. Pack pickles in hot sterilized jars. Wipe jar rims clean and seal at once with sterilized rings and lids. Yield: 7 to 8 pints.

Grapefruit Marmalade

3 white grapefruit (1 pound each)
2 lemons
3 cups water
1 box fruit pectin
10 cups sugar

Remove rind from fruit in quarters; lay flat and shave off about half of the white part; discard. Slice remaining peel into very thin strips. Place peel and water in a heavy pan and bring to boil. Reduce and simmer, covered, 20 minutes or until peel is tender. Chop peeled fruit, discarding seeds, and place pulp and juice into heavy pan with peel. Simmer, covered, 10 minutes. Mix fruit pectin with peel. Bring quickly to a hard boil, stirring constantly. Add sugar; bring to a full rolling boil. Boil hard 1 minute, stirring constantly. Remove from heat; skim off foam with a metal spoon. Pour into hot, sterilized jars, leaving ½-inch space at top. Wipe any spills from jar rim and immediately pour ⅛-inch hot paraffin on top. Yield: 10 half-pints.

Canning and Freezing

Strawberry Jam

2 quarts fully ripe strawberries, washed and drained
1 box fruit pectin
4 cups sugar
Paraffin

Crush berries with a potato masher or plate, one layer at a time, so that all berries are reduced to pulp. Place berries in a very large, heavy-bottomed saucepan. Stir pectin into pulp. Bring quickly to a full, hard boil, stirring constantly. Stir in sugar; bring back to a full rolling boil that is impossible to stir down and boil hard for 1 minute, continuing to stir constantly. Remove from heat; skim foam with metal spoon. Ladle into hot, sterilized jars, leaving ½-inch space at top. Wipe spills from rim of jar. Cover at once with ⅛-inch melted paraffin. Yield: 8 ½-pint jars.

Zucchini Pickles

2 cups vinegar
2 teaspoons dill seed
¾ cup sugar
1 teaspoon celery seed
¼ cup pickling salt
1 teaspoon turmeric
½ teaspoon ground mustard
2 quarts unpeeled zucchini, sliced into rings
1 quart onions, sliced into rings

Place everything except vegetables in a heavy kettle; bring to a boil. Pour over zucchini and onion and let stand approximately 1 hour. Place again in heavy kettle; bring to a boil; reduce heat and simmer 3 minutes. Pack at once into hot, sterilized jars to within ⅛-inch from the top. Wipe jar rim clean and seal at once with sterilized ring and lid. Repeat with remaining pickles. Yield: 3 pints.

Pumpkin Preserves

4 pounds raw pumpkin, finely diced
6 cups sugar
3 lemons, sliced very thin
4 teaspoons grated gingerroot

Pour 3 cups sugar over pumpkin and let stand, covered, overnight. The next day, add remaining sugar and bring to boil in a heavy kettle. Reduce heat and simmer 1¼ hours. Add lemon slices and ginger. Simmer 1 hour more. Pack into hot, sterilized jars, leaving ½-inch space at top. Wipe any spills from jar rims and immediately pour ⅛-inch hot paraffin on preserves. Yield: 8 half-pint jelly glasses.

Fresh Mint Jelly

1½ cups fresh mint leaves and stems, firmly packed
2¼ cups water
Juice of 1 lemon (2 tablespoons), strained
Green food coloring, optional
3½ cups sugar
½ bottle or 1 1¾-ounces box fruit pectin

Wash mint leaves and stems thoroughly. Place in a large saucepan and crush with a potato masher or glass. Add water and bring quickly to a boil. Remove from heat, cover, and let stand 10 minutes. Strain and measure 1¾ cups into saucepan. Add lemon juice and a few drops of food color if desired. Add sugar. Mix well. Place over high heat and bring to a boil, stirring constantly. Stir in fruit pectin. Bring back to a full rolling boil and boil hard for 1 minute, stirring constantly. Remove from heat, skim off foam with metal spoon, and pour quickly into sterilized jars or jelly glasses, leaving ½-inch space at top. Wipe any spills from jar rim and immediately pour ⅛-inch hot paraffin on jelly. Yield: 3¼ cups.

Bittersweet Orange Marmalade

6 medium-size, thin-skinned oranges
2 lemons
2 medium-size, thin-skinned grapefruit
2 cups water
7 cups sugar

Cut whole fruits into ⅛-inch slices, discarding seeds. Cut grapefruit slices into eighths; cut orange and lemon slices into quarters. Combine chopped fruit with water in a large, heavy saucepan. Bring to boiling point, then reduce heat and simmer, covered, until peel is tender and translucent, about 25 to 30 minutes. Add sugar to the pan and stir until dissolved. Increase heat to medium-high and cook, uncovered, stirring often. Boil about 30 minutes or until 2 drops of marmalade run together and sheet off the edge of a cold, metal spoon. Cover and let stand at room temperature for 24 hours. The next day, rapidly return marmalade to boiling, stirring constantly. Skim off any foam with a metal spoon and pour immediately into hot, sterilized jars, leaving ½-inch space at top. Wipe spills from rims and cover at once with ⅛-inch hot paraffin. Yield: approximately 10 half-pints.

One-Day-at-a-Time Pickles

    1 quart small, fresh pickling cucumbers
    2 quarts iced water
    1 cup cider vinegar
 1½ tablespoon kosher salt
    1 cup water
    4 cloves garlic, peeled and sliced
    1 teaspoon pickling spices (without red pepper)
    3 large heads fresh dill or 3 teaspoons dill seed

Place unscrubbed, firm cucumbers in iced water for 30 minutes. Scrub off dirt and remove any particles of blossoms. Meanwhile, sterilize one quart jar and lid. In a small, stainless steel pan, bring vinegar, salt, water, garlic, and pickling spices, to a boil. When mixture boils, remove garlic and place cucumbers in sterile jar with dill, packing carefully, so no cucumbers will touch the lid. Pour vinegar solution over cucumbers to within ½-inch of the top of the jar, wipe rim of jar, seal, and process in a boiling water bath for 10 minutes. Store jar in a dark place for at least 2 weeks before serving. Yield: 1 quart.

Note: Recipe can be multiplied by the amount of cucumbers harvested.

Mom's Dilled Zucchini Slices

    2 to 3 pounds fresh, firm zucchini
         about 4¾-inches long
 ¼ cup salt
    2 teaspoons celery seed
    2 teaspoons mustard seed
    4 cloves garlic
 2½ cups water
 2½ cups cider vinegar
    1 cup sugar
 ¼ cup salt
    4 heads fresh dill or 1 tablespoon dill seed

Wash zucchini and cut lengthwise into thin slices. Cover with 1-inch water and ¼ cup salt. Let stand for 2 hours. Drain thoroughly. Tie celery and mustard seed with garlic in a cheescloth bag. In a large saucepan, combine water, vinegar, sugar, and salt; add the spice bag and bring to a boil. Remove from heat and add zucchini slices. Let stand another 2 hours. Bring all ingredients to a boil and cook for five minutes. Place dill in the bottom of 4 sterilized pint jars. Place slices and brine in the jars, leaving ¼-inch at the top. Seal and process 10 minutes in a hot water bath. Yield: 4 pint jars.

Note: These are delicious to use fresh, too.

Julia's Rhubarb Chutney

    2 cups cider vinegar
    4 cups brown sugar
    4 cups chopped rhubarb
    4 cups chopped onion
    1 teaspoon salt
    1 teaspoon cinnamon
 ½ teaspoon ground allspice
 ½ teaspoon ground cloves
 ¼ teaspoon freshly ground black pepper
 ¼ cup finely chopped gingerroot

Combine vinegar and brown sugar in a heavy saucepan. Bring to a boil, reduce heat and simmer 5 minutes. Add remaining ingredients and simmer, covered, until fairly thick. Pour into hot, sterilized jars; wipe spills off jar rims and seal immediately with sterilized lids and rings. Yield: approximately 4 pints.

Mom's Beet Relish

    4 cups cooked or canned beets, drained
    1 cup cider vinegar
 ½ cup brown sugar, firmly packed
 ¼ cup grated horseradish
    1 teaspoon salt

Chop beets very fine. Place all ingredients in a saucepan and bring to a boil. Pour immediately into two sterilized pint jars and seal (or cool and serve). Yield: 2 pints.

Canned Tomatoes

   20 pounds (approximately) firm, ripe tomatoes
         (1 pound equals 4 small, 3 medium,
         or 2 large tomatoes)
    7 teaspoons salt
    7 tablespoons lemon juice

Plunge tomatoes into boiling water for 15 seconds, then plunge into ice water. Remove and peel. Leave whole or quarter. Fill sterilized jars with the tomatoes, pressing down until they yield juice and fill in the spaces. Fill to within ½-inch of the top. Run a knife down side of jars in several places to remove air bubbles. Add salt and lemon juice to each quart. Wipe rims and seal jars, tightening bands securely. Place jars on the rack in hot water bath, covered by one or two inches of water. Cover and bring to boiling. Boil gently for 45 minutes. Remove jars and place on wire racks to cool. Check seals. (Use those which don't seal as soon as possible; keep refrigerated.) Store in a cool, dark, dry place. Yield: 7 quarts.

Timesaving Basic Mixes

Why do so many of us buy prepackaged cake mixes, pie crusts, baking powder biscuits, salad mixes, baked goods, etc.? Because they save us time. But they generally don't save us money. Basic mixes, prepared at home, make baking fast and inexpensive.

Basic Quick Bread Mix

- 9 cups sifted, unbleached flour or 10 cups whole wheat pastry flour
- ⅓ cup baking powder
- 1 teaspoon cream of tartar
- 1 tablespoon salt
- 2 cups shortening

Stir together dry ingredients thoroughly. Sift into a very large bowl. Cut in shortening with a pastry blender until the mixture resembles coarse cornmeal. Store in an airtight container in the refrigerator. Do not pack down. Use as called for in the recipes that follow. Yield: approximately 13 cups mix.

Muffins

- 3 cups Basic Quick Bread Mix
- 2 tablespoons firmly packed brown sugar
- 1 cup milk
- 1 egg, beaten

Preheat oven to 425°. Place Mix and sugar in a medium-size mixing bowl. Stir until well blended. Make a well in the center of the ingredients and pour milk and egg into it. Stir until dry ingredients are just moistened. Fill muffin papers or greased muffin tins about one-half full with batter. Bake for about 20 minutes or until done. Yield: 12 muffins.

Variations: For blueberry muffins, apple muffins, or other fruit muffins, stir 1 cup of desired drained fruit (chop apples and similar fruit) into the muffin batter just before pouring into muffin tins.

Applesauce Bread

- 3 cups Basic Quick Bread Mix
- ½ cup brown sugar, firmly-packed
- 1 teaspoon cinnamon
- 1 cup thick applesauce
- ½ cup milk
- 1 egg, beaten

Preheat oven to 350°. Grease a 9 x 5 x 3-inch loaf pan thoroughly. Blend Mix, sugar, and applesauce together. Combine milk and egg and stir into applesauce mixture. Stir until well blended. Bake 1 hour or until done. Yield: 1 loaf.

Upside-Down Coffee Cake

- 2 cups Basic Quick Bread Mix
- ¼ cup plus ⅔ cup firmly packed brown sugar
- 1 teaspoon cinnamon
- ¼ cup chopped nuts
- 1 egg
- ½ cup milk, approximately
- 1 teaspoon vanilla
- ¼ cup margarine

Place Mix, ¼ cup brown sugar, cinnamon, and nuts into a bowl and mix thoroughly. Break egg into a measuring cup and add enough milk to make ¾ cup total. Add vanilla, and stir wet ingredients in measuring cup with a fork. Add to the dry ingredients. Stir until thoroughly blended. Preheat oven to 375°. Melt margarine in the bottom of an 8 x 8 x 2-inch cake pan. Stir in remaining sugar, and spread mixture evenly over bottom of pan. Pour batter over margarine mixture carefully and bake 30 minutes or until done. Remove coffee cake immediately from tin by loosening from sides of pan with a knife and inverting onto serving plate. Yield: 12 servings.

Banana Bread

- 3 cups Basic Quick Bread Mix
- ½ cup honey
- 1 cup mashed, ripe bananas
- 2 eggs, well beaten
- ½ cup nuts, optional

Preheat oven to 350°. Grease a 9 x 5 x 3-inch loaf pan thoroughly. Blend Mix, honey, and bananas together. Stir in eggs until well blended. Bake for 1 hour or until done. Yield: 1 loaf.

Banana Bread
Basic Quick Bread Mix
Apple Cider Bread p.5
Muffins

Waffles

1½ cups Basic Quick Bread Mix
2 teaspoons honey
1 egg, separated
1 cup milk

Blend mix, honey, beaten egg yolk, and milk. Beat egg white until stiff and fold in. Pour into prepared waffle iron and bake according to manufacturer's specifications. Yield: 5 waffles.

Pancakes

1½ cups Basic Quick Bread Mix
1 tablespoon honey
¾ cup milk
¼ cup raw wheat germ
1 egg, well beaten

Place mix into a bowl and stir in rest of the ingredients until well blended. Drop batter from a large spoon onto lightly greased, hot griddle. Turn once and serve. Yield: 1 dozen pancakes.

Streusel Topped Apple Bread

3 cups Basic Quick Bread Mix
¼ cup firmly packed brown sugar
1 teaspoon cinnamon
½ teaspoon cloves
2 eggs
¼ cup milk
5 cups chopped apples
½ cup raisins

Preheat oven to 375°. Mix together Mix, brown sugar, cinnamon, and cloves. Beat in eggs thoroughly for at least 1 minute. Stir in milk and blend thoroughly. Add apples and beat 1 more minute. Finally, stir in raisins. Pour batter into a well-greased 9 x 5 x 3-inch loaf pan. Spoon Streusel Topping evenly onto bread batter. Bake for about 1 hour or until done. Yield: 1 loaf.

Streusel Topping

⅔ cup brown sugar
½ cup unbleached flour
2 teaspoons nuts
1 teaspoon raw wheat germ
½ teaspoon cinnamon
¼ teaspoon salt
3 tablespoons cold margarine

Stir together, brown sugar, flour, nuts, wheat germ, cinnamon, and salt. Cut in margarine with a pastry blender until mixture resembles crumbs.

Baking Powder Biscuits

2 cups Basic Quick Bread Mix
½ cup milk

Preheat oven to 450°. Place mix in a bowl and make a well in the center. Add the milk and stir with fork until mix is well moistened. Form into a ball and turn out onto lightly floured surface. Knead lightly until smooth. Roll out with a floured rolling pin to ½-inch thickness and cut into 2-inch rounds. Place on lightly greased baking sheet and bake 15 minutes or until done. Yield: 1 dozen biscuits.

Note: For drop biscuits, do not knead but simply drop dough by the spoonful onto greased baking sheet and bake.

Quick Pizza

2 cups Basic Quick Bread Mix
⅓ cup milk
2 cups tomato sauce
1 teaspoon oregano
½ teaspoon sweet basil
1 clove garlic, minced
¼ cup minced onion
1 cup shredded mozzarella cheese
¼ cup grated Parmesan or Romano cheese
    Toppings: anchovies, green peppers, browned ground beef, pastrami, olives

Preheat oven to 425°. Stir milk and Mix together in a small bowl until dough forms. Turn onto a lightly floured board and knead lightly. Roll out dough with a well-floured rolling pin and place on a well-greased, 14-inch baking sheet. Turn up edges of dough to hold in filling. Mix together tomato sauce, oregano, garlic, and onion and spread onto dough evenly. Add favorite topping either before or after sprinkling on cheese, as desired. Bake 10 to 15 minutes or until crust is done. Yield: One 14-inch pizza.

Karin's Pumpkin Dessert

    1 cup Basic Quick Bread Mix
    ½ cup old-fashioned rolled oats
    ⅔ cup brown sugar, firmly packed
    ¼ cup plus 2 tablespoons firm margarine
    2 cups pumpkin puree (16-ounce can)
    1 13-ounce can evaporated milk
    2 eggs
    1 cup brown sugar
    ½ teaspoon salt
    1 teaspoon cinnamon
    ½ teaspoon ginger
    ¼ teaspoon cloves
    ⅔ cup chopped nuts

Preheat oven to 350°. Mix together Basic Mix, oats, ⅔ cup brown sugar, and ¼ cup margarine until crumbly. Press into a 10 x 13-inch baking pan. Bake 8 minutes. Beat together pumpkin, milk, eggs, sugar, salt, cinnamon, ginger, and cloves. Pour over hot oat mixture and bake fifteen minutes. Mix nuts and remaining brown sugar, and margarine. Sprinkle over hot pumpkin mixture and bake 15 to 20 minutes, or until knife inserted in the center comes out clean. Cool and serve with Spiced Whipped Cream, if desired. Yield: 12 to 16 servings.

Spiced Whipped Cream

    1 cup whipping cream
    1 tablespoon sugar
    1 teaspoon grated orange rind
    ½ teaspoon cinnamon

Chill cream, beaters, and bowl. Beat cream until as thick as desired. Stir in sugar and flavorings. Serve immediately.

Applesauce-Bran Cookies

    3 cups Basic Quick Bread Mix
    1 cup bran flakes
    1 cup firmly packed brown sugar
    ½ teaspoon allspice
    ½ teaspoon nutmeg
    1 teaspoon cinnamon
    1 teaspoon vanilla
    2 eggs, beaten
    1 cup thick applesauce
    ½ cup raisins or currants

Preheat oven to 350°. Mix dry ingredients together thoroughly. Stir in vanilla, eggs, applesauce, and, finally, raisins. Drop by teaspoonfuls onto well-greased baking sheets. Bake for 15 minutes or until done. Yield: 4 dozen cookies.

Basic Pastry Mix

    12 cups sifted, unbleached flour (or half whole
        wheat pastry flour)
    1½ tablespoons salt
    4 cups shortening

Sift flour with salt into a very large bowl. Cut in shortening with a pastry blender or fork until the mixture is the consistency of coarse cornmeal. Store in a tightly covered container in a cool place. Yield: 18 cups (about nine 2 crust 8-inch pies).

Pie Crust

Using the chart, measure required amount of Basic Pastry Mix into a bowl. Sprinkle water in slowly, tossing mixture with a fork. When dough is just moistened, form into a ball. Divide in half if for two crusts, and place half on a well-floured cloth. With a well-floured rolling pin, roll the crust into a circle extending at least an inch beyond outside edge of pan. Fit pastry into pan gently. Fill with desired filling and repeat directions for top crust. Press edges together. Flute edge of pie shell. For baked, unfilled pastry shell, prick bottom of crust with fork and bake at 425° for 10 to 12 minutes.

Size of Crust	Ice Water (Tablespoons)	Pastry Mix (Cups)
one 8-inch	1-2	1¼
two 8-inch	2-3	2
one 9-inch	2-3	1½
two 9-inch	3-4	2¾

Note: Measure pie pan from inside rim to inside rim. The typical 9-inch pie pan holds about 4 cups filling; and 8-inch pan typically holds about 3 cups. Tart shells can be baked in muffin tins.

Make and freeze extra pie crust shells; they'll be like store-bought but at much less expense.

Large cannisters, coffee cans, or restaurant-size mayonnaise or mustard jars can be perfect storage places for basic mixes.

To prevent hard pieces of brown sugar from forming, store in an airtight container with a slice of apple. This will keep the sugar moist. In order to salvage your purchase, use a grater to break down any hardened pieces of brown sugar.

Welsh Lemon Tarts

    5 cups Basic Pastry Mix
    7 tablespoons ice water
    4 tablespoons margarine
    1/3 cup brown sugar, firmly packed
    2 large egg yolks
    1 tablespoon grated lemon rind
    2 teaspoons brandy
    1/8 teaspoon salt
    1 1/2 cups small curd cottage cheese
    1/3 cup currants
        Whipped cream, optional

Place Pastry Mix into a mixing bowl. Sprinkle water over and toss with a fork. Form a ball from dough; knead lightly. Divide into two parts and roll out half on a lightly floured board with a floured rolling pin. With a 3½-inch cookie cutter or jar lid, cut dough into eight rounds. Press rounds gently into muffin tins or fluted tart pans. Repeat to make 16 tart shells. Preheat oven to 425°. In a small bowl, beat margarine until soft with an electric mixer. Beat in sugar until light and fluffy; add yolks, rind, brandy, and salt. Beat thoroughly. Stir in cottage cheese and beat until mixture is almost smooth. Finally, add currants. Spoon mixture into pastry shells. Bake for 10 minutes and lower heat to 350°. Bake 15 to 20 minutes more or until filling is golden. Cool completely on wire racks before carefully removing from tins. Serve with whipped cream, if desired. Yield: 16 tarts.

Cheese Appetizers

    2 cups Basic Pastry Mix
    1/2 teaspoon garlic powder
    1 tablespoon baking powder
    1 cup grated Parmesan or Romano cheese
    1/2 cup milk
        Flour

Mix dry ingredients together thoroughly. Add milk and stir—mixture will be sticky. Stir until mixture cleans the bowl. Preheat oven to 400°. Turn out onto a very well-floured board. Roll mixture into a ball on floured surface until workable. Roll out with a well-floured rolling pin until ¼-inch thick. Cut into strips, approximately 1 x 3-inches. Place strips on well-greased baking sheets and bake approximately 10 minutes or until lightly browned. Serve hot as an appetizer or cold as a snack or with soup. Can be frozen and reheated in aluminum foil, if desired. If stored, keep in a tightly covered tin. Yield: 4 dozen "sticks."

Basic White Sauce Mix

    2 2/3 cups non-instant powdered milk
    1 1/2 cups unbleached or whole wheat flour
        (or a combination)
    2 teaspoons salt
    1 cup margarine
        Freshly ground black pepper

Mix together milk, flour, and salt. Cut in margarine with a pastry blender until mixture resembles crumbs. Refrigerate in a tightly covered container until needed. To make 1 cup sauce, pour 1 cup cold milk into a small, heavy-bottomed pan. Thoroughly stir in ½ cup of the mix. Stir over medium heat until mixture is thickened and bubbly. Taste and correct seasonings. Use as is or in any recipe calling for a white or cream sauce. Yield: mix for 12 cups sauce.

Quick Spinach-Stuffed Zucchini

    1 very large or 2 medium-size zucchini
    1 10-ounce package frozen spinach
    1/2 cup White Sauce
    1/8 teaspoon nutmeg
        Salt
        Freshly ground black pepper
    1/4 cup grated Parmesan cheese

Slice zucchini in half lengthwise; steam until barely tender. Scoop out pulp and reserve. Preheat oven to 350°. Steam spinach until thoroughly hot; drain. Gently stir in white sauce and pulp from zucchini, adding nutmeg and salt and pepper, if needed. Spoon creamed spinach mixture into zucchini and sprinkle with Parmesan cheese. Place on greased baking sheet or in a casserole. Bake 30 minutes or until heated through. Yield: 4 servings.

To add inexpensive protein to a recipe calling for milk, mix in a tablespoon of nonfat dry milk powder, per cup of milk; there will be no change in the outcome of the recipe. To an appropriate recipe calling for water, consider adding ¼ to ½ cup nonfat dry milk per cup of water.

Timesaving Basic Mixes

Flaked Coconut, Coconut Cream, and Coconut Milk

1 coconut

With an ice pick and hammer, punch a hole in two of the coconut eyes. Drain the liquid and reserve. Crack the coconut shell into four or five pieces. If meat will not come out of the shell easily, place, shell side down, over electric burner set at low heat for about one minute. Protect hands with a potholder or towel, and lift the meat from the shell. Scrape away the thin, dark layer with a vegetable peeler. Cut the meat into cubes and place them in a blender or food processor. Pour the reserved coconut liquid over the coconut meat with two cups very hot water. Blend until meat is flaked as desired. Pour liquid out of blender through a sieve. Press to extract as much liquid as possible. This is coconut cream. Refrigerate. Pour another cup of hot water over flaked coconut and sieve again. The thinner liquid is coconut milk. Use cream or milk immediately or within 24 hours. Freeze coconut or liquid if not using right away. Yield: 2 cups flaked coconut, 2 cups cream, 1 cup milk.

Indonesian Dessert

2 tablespoons soft margarine or butter
2/3 cup sugar
6 tablespoons sifted, unbleached flour
1 teaspoon cinnamon
1/8 teaspoon salt
6 eggs, separated
1 1/2 cups coconut cream
4 tablespoons coconut
Whipped Cream, optional

Preheat oven to 350°. Cream butter and sugar together thoroughly. Stir in flour, cinnamon, and salt. Add egg yolks, one at a time, beating thoroughly after each addition. Gradually stir in Coconut Cream. Beat egg whites until stiff but not dry and fold into yolk mixture. Pour custard into buttered 2-quart baking dish. Sprinkle Coconut on top. Set dish in a larger, shallow pan of hot water so that the water comes a little more than halfway up the side of the baking dish. Bake until set, about 45 minutes. Serve chilled with whipped cream, if desired. Yield: 12 servings.

Economical Yogurt

1 1/2 cups instant nonfat dry milk
Lukewarm water (120°)
3 tablespoons good quality plain yogurt (commercial or homemade), fresh

Place dry milk in a sterilized quart jar. Blend in 1 cup lukewarm water. When thoroughly mixed, fill the container almost to the neck with additional lukewarm water. Stir well. Finally, stir in yogurt gently but thoroughly. Place plastic wrap on lip of jar and put cover on. Wrap well in several towels and place somewhere warm for 6 to 8 hours. Do not disturb for at least 6 hours, then check to see if it is thick as pudding. Yield: 1 quart, 2 pints, 4 cups.

Alternative Methods: Use yogurt maker, following directions. Or, in an oven that will maintain an even 115°, place the milk mixture into smaller sterilized jars such as baby food jars, cover and place in a pan filled to the jar necks with 115° water; leave in oven until yogurt is of desired consistency. Other incubators are an electric saucepan or frying pan that can keep an even low temperature no higher than 120°, or the pilot light on a gas stove.

Cucumber, Tomato, and Yogurt Salad

2 cups plain yogurt
1 large cucumber, chopped
2 ripe tomatoes, chopped
6 to 8 scallions, chopped
Freshly ground black pepper to taste
1/2 teaspoon cumin seed
Salt to taste
Dash of cayenne pepper, optional
Paprika

Beat yogurt until smooth. Toast cumin seed for 2 to 3 minutes in a heavy frying pan and crush. Stir cucumber, tomatoes, scallions, black pepper, and a pinch of cumin into yogurt; add salt to taste. Add cayenne if desired. Garnish with paprika and another pinch of cumin. Chill until ready to serve. Yield: 6 servings.

The Cook's Helpers

Glossary

Blanch
to drop slowly into boiling water for a few minutes then immediately place in ice water to stop cooking process; time varies with the vegetable. Pour boiling water over tomatoes and similar fruits and vegetables to make removal of skins easier.

Braise
to brown meat in vegetable oil and simmer, covered, with a small amount of additional liquid.

Mince
to cut up into very fine, tiny pieces.

Non-hydrogenated foods
foods which have not been processed with hydrogen to turn oil content into solid fat. Non-hydrogenated peanut butter can be recognized by the oil which rises to the top.

Non-instant powdered milk
more nutritious than instant.

Nutritional yeast
another name for brewer's yeast; an inexpensive source of protein and vitamin B complex. Can be consumed raw (in salads, juice, etc.), unlike baking or active yeast.

Old-fashioned molasses
unsulphured, dark molasses.

Puree
to mash cooked fruits or vegetables into a pulp, usually in a blender or sieve.

Sauté
to cook quickly in a small amount of oil, stirring or turning frequently.

Simmer
to cook just below boiling point; bubbles rise gently to the surface.

Unbleached flour
creamy white flour which has not been bleached with chemicals.

Wheat germ
part of the grain from which the new plant grows. Raw wheat germ contains high quality protein and B vitamins. Can be used in cooking process or sprinkled raw on a variety of foods.

Whole wheat flour
flour ground from the whole grain, containing endosperm, bran, and germ; milled from hard wheat.

Whole wheat pastry flour
more finely ground than whole wheat flour; milled from soft wheat.

Dollar-Saving Substitutions

Veal
chicken or turkey breast in many recipes

Ham
picnic ham or a meaty ham bone, if applicable

Beef tenderloin and similar cuts
ground chuck in many recipes

Ground beef
ground turkey or lamb in many recipes; substitute ground pork for some of the ground beef; try ground, cooked soy-beans, pinto beans, lentils, etc. as a substitute

Canned salmon
canned mackerel in many recipes

Ground cloves
allspice

Mace
nutmeg

Raisins
dates, currants, dried elderberries

Walnuts
ground roasted peanuts, hickory nuts (pick them yourself), and any other nuts at a lower cost or that can be harvested.

1 cup buttermilk
1 cup yogurt, 1 cup milk plus 1 tablespoon vinegar (in baked goods)

1 cup sour cream
1 cup plain yogurt in many recipes

Sharp Cheddar cheese
mild Cheddar, Colby, Longhorn

1 quart milk
1⅓ cup nonfat dry milk plus 3¾ cups cold water (for added nutrition at a low cost, use more dry milk)

1 tablespoon fresh herb
1 teaspoon dried herb

Hints: A Baker's Dozen

Thirteen Budget Saving Hints

1. Start "shopping the ads." Every week, check the newspaper ads from several super-markets that have the best prices throughout the store. If the prices are right, plan complete menus around the week's meat and other specials.

2. Shop when there is time to compare prices, sizes, and brands. Use a well-organized, thorough shopping list.

3. Clip and save coupons regularly—but only for products ordinarily purchased. When a local store offers double-coupon savings, it's almost always best to shop there that week. Keep a large envelope handy for coupons received in the mail or clipped from magazines and newspapers; before doing the weekly shopping, always look through the envelope to see which can be used.

4. Watch at the check-out counter to make certain charges are correct—particularly when the clerk has to figure out the cost of one item when it is priced in multiples, for example, 6 for 98¢. When buying all 6, be certain to stack them together.

5. Unbranded foods can be as nutritious as name brands, but ingredients may not be as uniform in size or color. Unbranded meat is USDA inspected, just as the regular meats on the counter are. In nearly every case, unbranded foods cost less than even store name brands.

6. Convenience foods are only that—convenient. The customer pays to have a machine do something he or she could just as easily do. Make bread crumbs, add almonds to green beans, glaze carrots, prepare salad dressings, instead of buying the prepacked product. Be certain to check the chapter "Timesaving Basic Mixes" in this cookbook.

7. Buy foods that are consumed in great quantity by the case near harvesttime when the store has a special and the price is low. Consider buying flour in 25-pound sacks and rice in the largest quantity that can be stored.

8. Slow cookers are more economical than the oven; the oven is more economical than stove burners in the use of energy.

9. Match the size of the saucepan with the electrical element on a stove. Whenever possible turn off the element before the food is totally cooked, and the stored-up heat (especially in heavy-bottomed saucepans) will finish the cooking without using energy. Don't overcook vegetables; they are less nutritious and money is wasted.

10. Try to use the oven to its fullest by cooking several dishes at the same time and then freezing those not needed for later. Try not to be an "oven peeper"—up to 20% of the heat is lost through frequent opening of the oven door.

11. Whenever possible, buy spices and herbs in bulk from a gourmet shop, specialty store, or health food store.

12. Budget-watchers should shop at garage sales, flea markets, etc., for kitchen utensils and pots and pans. Someone else's second-hand cast-iron utensils will be another person's treasures. Cast-iron frying pans and the like should be "seasoned" before using if they have not been taken care of properly in the past. This is done by scouring the utensil thoroughly, rinsing well, drying, and then greasing well with an unsalted oil. Heat the utensil in a hot oven for 20 to 30 minutes.

13. USDA "Good" meats are just as nutritious as "Choice" grades of meat. "Good" meats have less fat, therefore are less tender, but actually have more protein per weight than higher-priced grades. Many of the less tender, but less expensive, cuts of meat can be prepared very successfully by moist-cooking (braising, pressure-cooking, stewing, etc.) Meat that costs more per pound may actually cost less if it has little bone.

Index

C 1
D 2
E 3
F 4
G 5
H 6
I 7
J 8
K 9
L 0
  1

64